DUPLICATE BRIDGE
Alfred Sheinwold

Dover Publications, Inc.
New York

Published in Canada by General Publishing Company, Ltd., 30 Lesmill Road, Don Mills, Toronto, Ontario.
Published in the United Kingdom by Constable and Company, Ltd.

This Dover edition, first published in 1971, is an unabridged republication of the 1967 edition of the work originally published in 1954 by the Sterling Publishing Company, Inc., New York, under the title *Third Book of Bridge: How to Bid and Play in Duplicate Tournaments*. This edition is published by special arrangement with the Sterling Publishing Company, Inc.

International Standard Book Number: 0-486-22741-3
Library of Congress Catalog Card Number: 75-156814

Manufactured in the United States of America
Dover Publications, Inc.
180 Varick Street
New York, N. Y. 10014

Table of Contents

SCORING IN DUPLICATE TOURNAMENTS

Game

300-point bonus for a non-vulnerable game.
500-point bonus for a vulnerable game.

Part Score

50 points for any part score bid and made.

Honors

Do NOT count honors in a match-point event.
Count honors if the final score is in total points.

All other scores are exactly the same as in rubber bridge.

THE MOST FREQUENT IRREGULARITIES
Insufficient Bid

If a player makes an insufficient bid, he must:

(a) Substitute the lowest sufficient bid in the same denomination. There is then no penalty at all. E.g. he bids one club over an earlier bid of one spade; no penalty for a correction to *two* clubs. OR

(b) Substitute any other sufficient bid. E.g. he bids one club over an earlier bid of one spade; and then corrects by bidding one notrump. The offender's partner must pass for the rest of the hand, but the offender may bid again if the bidding gives him any further chances. OR

(c) Pass. The offender's partner must then pass for the rest of that hand. If an opponent becomes declarer, he may demand or forbid the lead of any specified suit. E.g. West bids one club over an earlier bid of one spade. He corrects by passing. East is barred for the rest of that hand. If South becomes declarer, he may say to West: "Lead a club," or "Don't lead diamonds," or the like. This demand or restriction applies only to the opening lead.

Call Out of Turn

A call out of turn is void. (A call is any bid, pass, double, or redouble.) The auction goes back to the player whose proper turn it was. Then:

(a) If the offense was a pass before any player has bid, or when it was the turn of the player on the offender's right, the offender must pass at his next turn. E.g. South deals, and West passes before anything else has been said. West must pass at his first turn, but he may bid later if he gets any further chances; and East may bid or pass as he pleases.

(b) If the offense is anything not listed in (a), the offender's partner must pass for the rest of that hand (but the offender himself may bid or not, as he pleases). E.g. North (dealer) one heart; South one spade. The spade bid is cancelled, and it is East's turn to bid. North must pass for the rest of the hand, but South may pass, bid, double, or redouble whenever it is his turn. South is not required to bid spades; he may, for example, jump to three notrump at his next turn.

Opening Lead Out of Turn

If the wrong defender makes the opening lead, declarer may:

(a) *Forbid the lead of that suit.* In this case, the card wrongly led is picked up. The correct defender leads *any* other suit, and play then proceeds normally. OR

(b) *Treat the card led as a penalty card.* The correct defender may lead any suit at all, and the card wrongly led is left face up on the table. That card must be played by the offender at the first legal opportunity. That is, the offender must play it as soon as the suit is led; or must discard it if another suit is led to which he cannot follow; or he must lead the card if he wins a trick before he has played the penalty card. OR

(c) *Condone the lead out of turn.* In this case, declarer announces his intention of condoning, and the dummy is put down. Declarer plays second to the trick, and the dummy plays last.

Declarer must announce his choice of the three courses before the play proceeds.

Always call the tournament director promptly whenever an irregularity occurs. Do NOT rely on your own memory of the rules.

HOW TO USE THIS BOOK

This book has been written for two kinds of players: those who have played duplicate bridge before and know the mechanics of the game, and those who know rubber bridge but are completely unfamiliar with duplicate. The first type of player can afford to skip the first chapter, being content to know that the information is there to refer to when and if he needs it. The second type of player should read the first chapter at some time, not necessarily first.

If you decide to begin with the second chapter (on the general principles of tournament play) and find yourself at a loss to understand any of the mechanical details, consult the index and find out where the point is covered—whether in the first chapter or in another place—and look it up. This is a ready-reference book as well as a (not too light) reading book.

Many tournament veterans use rubber bridge tactics in duplicate games without being aware that the two games are very different. Once you have become familiar with the inner philosophy of duplicate bidding and play, you will be able to separate the games in your mind and gain the utmost pleasure from being at home in both fields.

1. The Mechanics of Duplicate Bridge

WHAT IS A DUPLICATE TOURNAMENT?

A duplicate tournament is a bridge contest in which each hand is fully bid and played at one table, after which the very same hand is bid and played by entirely different people at another table. Everything except the players remains the same: the cards, the position of the dealer, the vulnerability—everything you can think of. The re-play *duplicates* the original conditions.

Perhaps you wonder how the same hand can be played more than once. It's really very easy, as you'll see when we come to it. First, let's go into the general advantages and attractions of duplicate, or tournament, bridge.

When you play ordinary rubber bridge you sometimes hold good cards and sometimes bad cards. It's hard for you to know whether you are playing well or badly. If the results are good, you glow with pride in your skill, when perhaps you should be thanking your rabbit's foot for bringing you such good cards!

If you are very modest, which is exceptional in a bridge player, you may act in the opposite way. You may believe that you have been lucky when you have really played well, and you may think that you have played badly when you have just been unlucky. The point is that it is very difficult to discover the truth in a game of ordinary rubber bridge.

There is no such difficulty in duplicate bridge. Somebody else always picks up and plays exactly the same cards that you get. If those cards are good, it is up to you to win more with them than the other fellow does; and if those cards are bad, your task is to lose less with them. The luck of the deal, so important at ordinary rubber bridge, simply *doesn't exist* in duplicate bridge.

Here's another important difference. In rubber bridge, you may play a hand at game or slam and go down. The thought crosses your mind that you may have muffed it, but then you go on to the next hand and you soon forget it and thus lose the chance to learn something from your mistake. In a duplicate game it is easy for you to look up the score of that hand to see what sort of result other players had with it. If several other players made the contract, it is clear that you made a mistake, and you can probably ask one of the successful declarers how he played it—and why. The average good player will be very happy to tell you all about his good plays, and you may thus learn a very useful lesson.

These advantages, attractive as they are, wouldn't make thousands of bridge enthusiasts play regularly in duplicate tournaments except for one all-important point: bridge tournaments are fascinating and exciting. They will improve your game, to be sure, but the important thing is that you'll enjoy yourself thoroughly while you learn.

Look up the nearest duplicate club (there are several thousand in the United States and Canada alone) and play in a few tournaments. Once you get the habit, nothing will stop you from playing. (If your bridge friends can't tell you where to find a nearby duplicate club, write to the American Contract Bridge League, 125 Greenwich Avenue, Greenwich, Conn. 06830.)

Incidentally, duplicate tournaments give you the chance to play against experts and to see for yourself how they bid and play. At the beginning, they will probably beat you, but this won't embarrass you because the experts will also beat many other players. All it can cost you is the entry fee, which is usually about the same as the price of a movie.

The purpose of the duplicate board, pictured above, is to make it easy for you to pass the 52 cards of a deal to another table with the four original hands intact. The board has four pockets, and each of the four original hands goes into one of those pockets. The board can then be passed from one table to another or even from one room to another without any risk of upsetting the arrangement of the cards.

Before we go into the way that cards are put into the board, let's take a closer look at the board itself. The best duplicate boards are made of wood or metal, a little longer than a business-sized envelope (about 10″x4″). One of the four pockets is marked DEALER.

Some of the pockets may be marked *vul.*, meaning that the players who hold those cards are vulnerable. In the best boards, the vulnerability is indicated not only by the *vul.* but also by the fact that the bottom of the pocket is painted red. Sometimes one partnership is vulnerable, sometimes the other; sometimes neither, sometimes both. This is always indicated by the *vul.* and by the red paint.

Many boards are used in a duplicate game, since in the course of an evening's play you would expect to bid and play about 25 to 30 hands. Each board is numbered to make it easy for you to tell one from another. The position of the dealer and the vulnerability differ from one board to another.

Each board has an arrow and the compass directions N, E, S, and W, standing for North, East, South, and West. The board is always put on each table in such a way that the arrow points to the "North" end of the room. (The tournament director always calls one end of the room "North," regardless of where true geographical North may happen to be.)

This arrangement makes it easy to tell one partnership from the other at each table in the tournament. One pair is called North-South because they play the North-South cards; and the other pair is called East-West.

SEAT ASSIGNMENTS

At the beginning of a duplicate game, the tournament director usually tells you and your partner where to sit. He may say "Take any East-West seats." You then look for any table at which the East-West seats are unoccupied, and you take those seats.

Sometimes the director will ask you to sit at a particular table. The tables are numbered, so it won't be hard to find the right place.

After you have played several times at the same club, you will probably know where to sit without being told. You may even be asked to take North-South seats, which will be an indication that you are considered experienced players. (One reason for this is that the North-South players keep the score, as we shall see, and a sensible tournament director will try to make sure that this job falls into experienced hands.)

THE SHUFFLE AND THE DEAL

Just before the game is scheduled to begin, the tournament director will put two or three duplicate boards on each table. Each board has cards in it; and you will find at least one card in each board turned face up, as a warning that the hand has not yet been shuffled and dealt. You are expected to shuffle the cards of each board, deal, and play. (After the game begins, of course, you don't pass the board to another table with any card face up.)

You take one board, remove the cards from it, shuffle them in the normal way, and deal the cards into four separate packets in front of you. Then you put one of these packets into each of the pockets of the board. This operation completes the shuffle and deal.

This is, as you can see, a very simple task, but it is possible to do something wrong even here. If your opponents are late in coming to the table, wait until they arrive before you shuffle and deal the cards. You might feel a bit suspicious if you arrived late, found the cards already shuffled and dealt, and if your opponents then bid and played the hands with unusually good luck.

Occasionally, in a club duplicate, there will be an odd number of pairs. When this happens, one pair sits out during each round of the duplicate. At the beginning, the odd pair will have no opponents to watch the shuffle and deal of the boards placed on that table. That pair should leave the boards untouched, to be shuffled by the players who will get those boards next.

Sometimes players who have no opponents for the first

round amuse themselves by stacking a freakish hand or a problem hand instead of shuffling and dealing in the normal way. This is about as amusing as putting a tack on somebody's chair. The best way to avoid even the suspicion of such childishness is to leave the boards alone with their revealing face-up cards, or to do the shuffling and dealing under the supervision of the tournament director.

It is customary to shuffle all of the boards before playing any of them. Each player can do one board, if necessary, and it is thus possible to shuffle and deal four boards just about as quickly as one. The boards are then stacked on top of each other in numerical order, with the arrow of each board pointing to the North end of the room.

THE BIDDING

Each player takes his cards out of the uppermost board and counts the cards face down. Make a habit of this from the very beginning of your tournament career. If you have exactly 13 cards, all is well. If you have too many or too few, the error may be corrected before any player has seen his cards.

Assuming that all goes well with the counting, the bidding begins with the player whose hand is labeled DEALER. He may bid or pass, exactly as though he had just dealt the hand in a normal game of rubber bridge.

The bidding then proceeds in the ordinary way. There is, however, one important difference. Even on the very first board one or both pairs may be vulnerable. In duplicate bridge your vulnerability comes *only from the marking on the duplicate board*—not from bidding and making a game on some earlier hand.

Another fact to remember is that part scores are not carried over from one hand to help you make a game on the next hand.

If you play in more than one club, you will find that all sets of duplicate boards have similar markings to indicate the dealer and the vulnerability. That is, you will be vulnerable about half of the time and dealer one quarter of the time.

HOW TO PLAY THE CARDS

After the bidding has ended in the normal way, the player to the left of the declarer makes the opening lead. The dummy is then exposed, just as in ordinary rubber bridge.

This may all sound just like rubber bridge, but there is an important difference. The opening lead is not put in the middle of the table; instead, it is left face up on the table very close to the player who led it. The middle of the table is occupied by two or three duplicate boards, which should remain stacked on the table throughout the play of the cards.

Declarer looks at the dummy, makes his plan for the play of the hand, and names the card that he wants played to the first trick. (Declarer is allowed to reach over and touch the card that he wants played, but it is customary merely to name the card.) The dummy picks up the card that has been named and holds it face up on the table very close to himself.

The leader's partner now plays a card. He, likewise, puts his card face up on the table very near to his own edge of the table. Finally, declarer plays a card in the same way—putting it face up on the table as near as possible to himself.

At this moment, all four cards of the first trick have been played. These four cards are not bunched together in the middle of the table, as in rubber bridge. Instead, each card is very near to the person who played it. It's just as easy, after a few minutes of practice, to see the four cards of a trick in four separate spots as it is to see them all together. Moreover, it's far easier to see exactly who played each card than it sometimes is in rubber bridge.

The player who won the trick leads to the second trick, and so on, just as in rubber bridge. Each trick is turned over in the same way—that is, each player turns over his own card and leaves it face down on the table in front of him.

At the end of a hand, each player has his original thirteen cards face down in front of him. He can easily put them face down into the same pocket of the duplicate board from which he originally took them. A very careful player counts his cards to make sure that he still has exactly thirteen before putting them back into the board.

You will naturally wonder: How do the players know which tricks were taken by each side?

As you turn down each card, you overlap it on the card of the previous trick as in the diagram opposite. You point a card towards yourself if your side won the trick; towards the opponents if they won the trick.

In the diagram, North-South have just won ten tricks at some contract. In each of the four hands, ten cards point in the North-South direction. The first, fifth, and eleventh cards point towards East-West, indicating that East-West won the first, fifth, and eleventh tricks. If the players were uncertain about any question of play, they could turn over all the cards in the exact order of their play, thus repeating the play of each trick.

You will sometimes see players who don't keep their cards in this careful and correct order. Instead, they may keep the tricks that they have won on one side and the tricks that they have lost on another side. There are even some players who nervously shuffle the cards of previous tricks while considering a lead or a play. It's just as easy for a beginner to get used to the *correct* method as to any incorrect method. You'll find that practically every leading player is careful to keep his cards in the correct order.

You may wonder why the duplicate boards are left in the middle of the table during the play of the cards. One reason is that the board indicates the dealer and the vulnerability. Also,

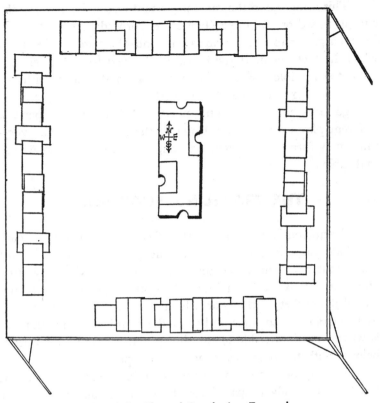

How the Played Cards Are Turned

it serves as a constant reminder to the players not to put their cards in the middle of the table.

There is never any problem if you have only two or three boards on the table. Four or more boards may make a pile that blocks your vision. It is quite all right in such a case to remove *some* of the boards from the table, provided that you always keep the *current* board on the table until the cards have been properly put back into the correct pockets.

This brings us to the most important reason for keeping the current board on the table. The correct procedure makes it easy for each player to put his cards back into the same pocket from which he took them. If the board is removed from the table, it is all too possible for it to be put back on the table with the arrow pointing South instead of North, in which case the cards will go back into the wrong pockets. When this happens, a different player will be the dealer at the next table, and everything may turn out differently through no fault of the player at that table.

THE TRAVELING SCORESLIP

When you have finished the play of a board in a club duplicate game, the North player enters the score on a slip of paper that has been folded inwards (to conceal what is written on it) and that has been inserted together with the cards into one of the pockets of the board. Each such slip is given a number that corresponds to the number of the board, and this number is written on the outside of the slip so that you can make sure it belongs with the board even before you open it up.

The slip of paper is a printed or mimeographed form that has been carefully prepared for the score at each table. Since this slip is kept inside a pocket of the board and travels with the board (as we shall see) from table to table, it is called a traveling scoreslip.

Let us suppose that you start the tournament in the East-West seats at Table 3. The director has put boards 5 and 6 on the table, and you have just finished playing board 5. You played the hand at two spades, making your contract with an overtrick.

The North player opens the traveling scoreslip and enters the score as indicated on this diagram:

OFFICIAL A.C.B.L. TRAVELING SCORE
[Mitchell]
NORTH PLAYER keeps score
ENTER PAIR NO. OF E-W PAIR   Board No. [5]

| N-S Pair | E-W Pair | FINAL CONTRACT PLAYED BY | NORTH - SOUTH | | N-S Match Points |
			Net Plus	Net Minus	
1 vs.					
2 vs.					
3 vs.	3	2S W		140	
4 vs.					
5 vs.					
6 vs.					
7 vs.					
8 vs.					
9 vs.					
10 vs.					
11 vs.					

The North player enters the score on line 3 because his pair number is 3. Your number is likewise 3, since both pairs take their number from the number of the original table. The difference is that you are 3 E-W, and your opponents are 3 N-S.

The North player puts your pair number down in the appropriate column. (At subsequent tables North will ask you for your pair number. You will remain "Pair 3" throughout the tournament.)

He writes the contract as 2 S W, which means two spades, played by West.

The next step is to record the points won or lost in the correct column. Since you played the hand and made your contract with an overtrick, the North player is minus. He is minus whenever his side plays the hand and goes down or whenever his opponents play the hand and make their contract.

The amount of the score is written as a single entry, since

there is no such thing as above-the-line or below-the-line scoring. You scored 60 points for making two spades, 30 points for the extra trick, and 50 points for a part score bid and made. The total is 140 points.

With very few exceptions, the scoring is the same in duplicate bridge as in rubber bridge. The major suits are 30 points per trick; the minors, 20. Doubles and redoubles affect the score just as they do in rubber bridge. Game is 100 points in trick score, as in rubber bridge. Penalties and bonuses for undertricks and overtricks are just what you're used to. Slam bonuses are the same. So is the bonus for making a doubled or redoubled contract.

What is different then? There are four differences:

1. You get a 50-point bonus for bidding and making any part score.

2. You get a 300-point bonus for bidding and making a non-vulnerable game.

3. You get a 500-point bonus for bidding and making a vulnerable game (regardless of whether or not the other side is vulnerable).

4. Honors are not scored. (Honors are counted in one kind of contest—total point team games. Forget about honors in the ordinary club duplicate game.)

MOVING FOR THE NEXT ROUND

When you have played all of the boards that were put on your table (usually two or three boards), you have finished the *round*.

The tournament director will have his eyes and ears open for signs that the round has been finished, and he will announce: "Next round, please."

In the ordinary club duplicate, all of the North-South players sit still throughout the session. The East-West players, however, move each round to the next higher numbered table. When they reach the highest numbered table, their next move is to Table 1. For example, if you start at Table 3, you go to Table 4 for the second round; and so on.

The boards also move at the end of each round, but they move in the *opposite* direction: to the next lower numbered table, and from Table 1 to the highest numbered table. For example, the boards that you played at Table 3 during the first round go to Table 2 for the second round; to Table 1 for the third round; and to the highest numbered table for the fourth round.

We now can understand why the tournament director prefers to let the experienced players sit North-South. Not only does the North player keep the score, but he also passes the boards, at the end of the round, to the next lower numbered table. This table is usually just behind the North player's back, but the North player at Table 1 may have to walk the length of the room to pass boards to the highest numbered table. (For this reason, the tables are often set up in the shape of the letter U, with the first and last tables fairly near each other at the open ends.)

The North-South players play the boards in numerical order. At Table 3, for example, they begin with boards 5 and 6; they play 7 and 8 on the second round, 9 and 10 on the third round, and so on. The North-South players are expected to know this and are expected also to sing out promptly for the tournament director if they are given the wrong boards by some mischance.

The East-West players skip one set of boards each round. It isn't necessary for you to know which boards you will play each round if you are East-West, since the North-South players are responsible for checking the boards before anybody takes cards out of a board. If you want to satisfy your curiosity, however, here's how it works: if you start with boards 5 and 6 at Table 3, you get boards 9 and 10 next at table 4 (skipping boards 7 and 8); you get boards 13 and 14 next at table 5 (skipping boards 11 and 12); and so on.

If you find that you are confused by all of these comments, put them out of your mind and come back to them when you have played a few sessions of duplicate. You will then find them surprisingly easy to understand. At the beginning all you need is the knack of moving from one table to the next higher table at the end of each round. You can leave the movement of the boards to the experienced players or to the tournament director.

THE PRIVATE SCORECARD

Every experienced duplicate player keeps a private scorecard. This may be a regular printed card, or it may be merely a traveling scoreslip converted for the moment into a private score. The idea is chiefly that you want a record of what you did on each board so that you can discuss the interesting hands later on with your partner or with other players.

Perhaps when you play board 5 you have the vague feeling that you should have made four spades instead of going down one. If you have a private score, you put a check mark opposite board 5 (or whichever board you're interested in) and look up the traveling scoreslip later on to see whether or not other players actually made four spades. Or perhaps you will find it simpler to ask other players what they did on board 5. If you didn't keep the private score you probably would forget all about board 5 (and the other problem hands) by the end of the session.

Another reason for keeping the private score is to have a reminder of what you did on each board in case some other player asks *you* whether or not you bid the slam on board so-and-so. Such discussions are half the fun of playing in duplicate games, in addition to which they are often highly instructive.

When you play in important tournaments, the private score enables you to make sure that you have been properly credited

Vul.	Bd. No.	vs.	Contract & Declarer	Plus	Minus	Pts. Est.	Pts.	Vul.	Bd. No.	vs.	Contract & Declarer	P
None	1							E-W	19			
N-S	2							Both	20			
E-W	3							N-S	21			
Both	4							E-W	22			
N-S	5		2S W	140				Both	23			
E-W	6		4S W		100			None	24			
Both	7							E-W	25			
None	8							Both	26			
E-W	9		3NT N		430			None	27			
Both	10		6S N		1430			N-S	28			
None	11		3H E	170				Both	29			
N-S	12		1NT S		120			None	30			
Both	13		3NT N	100				N-S	31			
None	14		4H x N	300				E-W	32			
N-S	15							None	33			
E-W	16							N-S	34			
None	17							E-W	35			
N-S	18							Both	36			

Check Your Score For Vulnerability

with the correct score on each board. It isn't necessary to check the scores in a club duplicate if you have been careful to look at the score on the traveling scoreslip after each hand to make sure that the North player has entered the correct amount in the correct place.

If you keep a private scorecard, as you should, enter the result of each hand in such a way that your opponents can't see what else is written on the card. It would be very embarrassing for them to see what score you had obtained on a board that they had not yet played. For the same reason, you never throw your private scorecard away during the middle of the game even if you are justly annoyed with it. Somebody else may pick it up and get information about a board that he still has to play.

WHY TOTALLING POINTS IS NOT ENOUGH

After a suitable number of rounds (determined in advance by the tournament director), the duplicate game comes to an end. The director gathers up all of the traveling scoreslips and retires to a corner of the room, where he performs mysterious operations on the slips to determine the final score of each pair. If you ask what is going on, you'll be told that the director is *match-pointing* the slips. Ask a foolish question and you get a foolish answer!

Before we go into the explanation of this mystery, here are a few general considerations. Let's suppose that in all of the boards most of the high cards were held by the North-South players. Naturally, most of the North-South players scored one game or slam after another. If you added up all of the points you had scored with the East-West cards, you wouldn't come close to the total amount scored by any of the North-South pairs. In fact, no East-West pair would have any chance to win from the North-South pairs.

Evidently, we have to find a better method of determining the *final* score of each pair.

Let's suppose that you compare your score on board 11 with another East-West pair. You find, of course, that they held the very same cards that you did on board 11. If you compare a few other scores, you find that this other East-West pair held exactly the same cards that you did on *every* board.

This gives you an idea. If you add up all of your scores and compare the total with any other *East-West* pair, the result will not depend on the luck of the deal.

You aren't particularly interested in the North-South players, but the same thing is true of them. All of the North-South pairs held exactly the same cards, and therefore they can discover the best North-South pair by adding up all the scores and finding out which pair has the highest total.

This method seems fairly simple and logical—and it is. It was used in duplicate games for many years, until the players became dissatisfied with one important defect—the fact that a few "big" hands determined the result for the entire session.

Suppose, for example, that one of the East-West pairs bids a gambling grand slam on board 19. Thanks to three finesses and a lucky suit break, the grand slam happens to be unbeatable. Nobody else is optimistic enough to bid even a small slam on the hand, so that the one ambitious East-West pair scores 1500 points (the grand slam bonus) on this hand that no other East-West pair earned. With this cushion of 1500 points, that East-West pair can afford to drop a trick here and there and to play rather sloppy bridge—yet still win by a handsome margin.

This is an extreme example, to be sure, but the total-point method of scoring emphasized the game and slam hands and left all the players indifferent to the part score hands. As a result, the players who bid and played skillfully throughout the session often found themselves beaten by pairs who had been lucky with just a few big hands.

It was necessary to look for still another way of determining the final score of the players. The match point method was the result of this search.

MATCH POINTS

The general principle of the match point method is very simple: each hand counts equally towards your final score, regardless of whether the hand will produce a grand slam, a small part score or even down two! When this method is used, you can't rely on a few big hands to pull you through; you have to play well on *all* of the hands.

In awarding match points on any board, the tournament director compares your score on that board with the score of each pair that played the board in the same direction. If you played the board as an East-West pair, your score is compared only with other East-West scores; if you played it North-South, your score is compared only with other North-South scores. The director gives you one match point for each such pair that you beat and one-half match point for each such pair that you tied.

Let's see how this works out with a typical traveling score-slip:

OFFICIAL A.C.B.L. TRAVELING SCORE
[Mitchell]
NORTH PLAYER keeps score
ENTER PAIR NO. OF E-W PAIR   Board No. [*1*]

N-S Pair	E-W Pair	FINAL CONTRACT PLAYED BY	NORTH - SOUTH		N-S Match Points
			Net Plus	Net Minus	
1 vs. 1		4S N	480		
2 vs. 3		4S N	450		
3 vs. 5		5S N	450		
4 vs. 7		4S N	420		
5 vs. 2		6S N		50	
6 vs. 4		3NT S	460		
7 vs. 6		5C×E	300		
8 vs.					
9 vs.					
10 vs.					
11 vs.					

The first thing to do is to award match points to the North-South pairs. After that has been completed, we'll give match points to the East-West pairs.

The best North-South score happens to be on the top line. Pair 1 N-S beat all the other N-S pairs on this board and therefore earn 6 match points, or 1 point for each pair.

Next-best are Pair 6 N-S, with 460. They have beaten five other pairs and therefore get 5 match points.

Our next award is a tie between Pair 2 N-S and Pair 3 N-S. One of them played the hand at four spades, and the other at five spades, but the result of 450 points is the same. They each beat three pairs and tied one pair, so they get 3½ match points each.

Pair 4 N-S get the next award—only 2 points, for beating just two pairs. Either this North player made a mistake or perhaps his opponents put up a brilliant defense, since he made no overtricks at all, while the pairs that we have already considered all made at least one overtrick.

Pair 7 N-S get only 1 match point, since they beat only one pair. Their opponents sacrificed against them, and Pair 7 could collect only 300 points by doubling five clubs. This is very bad for poor Pair 7, but very good for their opponents (Pair 6 E-W).

Finally, we come to Pair 5 N-S, who beat nobody at all. They therefore get a zero. This is sometimes called a *bottom,* and the best score on the board is usually called a *top.* As you can see, Pair 5 ambitiously bid a slam on the hand and went down one trick. Since nobody else tried for this slam, the chances are that it was a poor gamble, and that Pair 5 will learn a lesson from this hand.

We now proceed to award match points to the East-West pairs. If we chose, we could do it by the same method. The best E-W score is plus 50 (note that every N-S minus is an E-W plus and vice versa), so that Pair 2 E-W get the top score of 6 points. The next best E-W score is minus 300, so that Pair 6 E-W get 5 match points. And we could continue the process to the end.

In practice, this isn't done. The best E-W score is always the worst N-S score, and vice versa. In order to obtain any E-W match point award, look at what their N-S opponents got, and subtract that from *top on the board.*

For example, take the E-W pairs in order, as they appear

on the scoreslip. Pair 1 E-W: Their opponents got 6 (which was top on the board). Subtract 6 from 6, and you get 0. Hence Pair 1 E-W get a zero.

Pair 3 E-W: Their opponents got 3½. Subtract this from 6, and you get 2½. Hence Pair 3 E-W get 2½ match points.

Pair 5 E-W: Their opponents likewise got 3½, and for the same reason Pair 5 get 2½.

Pair 7 E-W: Their opponents got 2. Subtract from 6, and you get 4. Hence Pair 7 get 4 match points.

Pair 2 E-W: Their opponents got 0. Subtract from 6, and you get 6. Hence Pair 2 get 6 match points (top score for E-W).

Pair 4 E-W: Their opponents got 5. Subtract from 6, and you get 1. Hence Pair 4 get 1 match point (next to bottom).

Pair 6 E-W: Their opponents got 1. Subtract from 6, and you get 5. Hence Pair 6 get 5 match points (next to top).

The illustration on the opposite page shows the scoreslip with the match points written in:

YOUR TOTAL SCORE

After the tournament director has matchpointed all of the traveling scoreslips, he adds up all of the match points that were scored by each of the pairs. The totals are usually posted on a blackboard or some such device.

How do you know when you have a good score? You don't expect to win your first duplicate game, but you should aim to get above *average*. This brings us to a new idea.

Let's take an example. Suppose you play in a 7-table game, with 28 boards in all. Top on any board is 6 match points, and average on any board is therefore 3 match points. (Top on a board is always 1 point less than the number of tables that play the board.) If you multiply average on a board (3 points) by the number of boards (28 boards), you get 84 match points— which is average for the session.

OFFICIAL A.C.B.L. TRAVELING SCORE
[Mitchell]
NORTH PLAYER keeps score
ENTER PAIR NO. OF E-W PAIR · Board No. **[1]**

N-S Pair	E-W Pair	FINAL CONTRACT PLAYED BY	NORTH - SOUTH		N-S Match Points
			Net Plus	Net Minus	
1 vs. 1		4SN	480		6
2 vs. 3		4SN	450		3½
3 vs. 5		5SN	450		3½
4 vs. 7		4SN	420		2
5 vs. 2		6SN		50	0
6 vs. 4		3NTS	460		5
7 vs. 6		5CxE	300		1
8 vs.					
9 vs.					
10 vs.					
11 vs.					
12 vs.					
13 vs.					
14 vs.					

E-W Match Points

1	0
2	6
3	2½
4	1
5	2½
6	5
7	4
8	
9	
10	
11	
12	
13	
14	

A. C. B. L. SUPPLIES, 33 West 60th St. New York 23
Form 244

• **The Mechanics of Duplicate Bridge** • **31**

How good is it to achieve an average score? It's no great feat if you're a very experienced player and if the game is only an ordinary club game. Average is a good goal, however, for an inexperienced player even in an ordinary club game. And it would be a very high goal, indeed, if you were playing in a national championship instead of in a club duplicate. In other words, the score you get depends partly on how strong the competition is.

Your score is sometimes expressed in percentage of top on every board. Average would be 50%. The duplicate is usually won by a score of slightly more than 60%. A score of 65% is unusually good, and 70% is really phenomenal.

Let us hope that you won't often discover how bad a 40% score is. Even good players can sometimes get such a score, particularly if they get desperate and try to pick up spilled milk. An inexperienced player may get less than 40%, but he shouldn't admit it.

Let's try a different number of tables and boards and see what these percentages mean. Suppose you are playing in a 9-table game, with 27 boards in all. (This would be 3 boards per table, just as 28 boards meant 4 boards per table in a 7-table game.) Top on any board is 8 points, or 1 point less than the number of tables. Average on a board is 4 points, and average for the session is 4 x 27, or 108 points. A score of 50% would be 108 points; 60% would be 129½, and 40% would be 86½ points. A score in the middle 130's should win or come close to winning; and a score of 150 (very nearly 70%) would be phenomenally good.

2. General Principles of Tournament Play

Most people who play duplicate bridge do so in order to pass the time pleasantly with a game that they enjoy. They have a fine time, and they bid and play in a duplicate game exactly as they would bid in a rubber bridge game. They are the salt of the earth. They never win.

The beginning of wisdom in match point duplicate is to know that it is a very different game from rubber bridge. There are fine rubber bridge players who can go through all the motions of playing in a duplicate game but rarely get above average. Likewise, there are tournament stars who are prize patsies whenever they play rubber bridge. Many of the elements of skill in bidding and play are the same for both games, but there are also many important differences. We'll discuss some of them now and others at appropriate moments in other chapters.

THE SCORING TABLE

In rubber bridge every game is worth roughly 500 points. If you sacrifice 500 points to stop the enemy's game, you feel that you have made an even trade.

In duplicate bridge, a non-vulnerable game is worth *exactly* 300 points plus the trick score. This may come to 400, or 420, or perhaps 460 points, depending on the contract and on the number of overtricks. The non-vulnerable game does *not* come to 500 points. Hence if your sacrifice bid costs 500 points against a non-vulnerable game, you have made a *disastrous* trade.

How can it be a disaster, you may ask, to give up 500 points when the opponents could have scored 460 points if you had kept quiet? The difference is only 40 points, after all. Such a small difference is meaningless at rubber bridge, but it is the sun, the moon, and half of the stars at duplicate bridge.

Suppose at all of the other tables the hand is played at three no-trump by North, for a score of 460 points for North-South. You, West, sacrifice at four clubs, which is doubled and set for a penalty of 500 points. You get no match points at all on this board. Every bottom score (like this one) is a disaster, whether you have earned the bottom by a narrow margin or by going down 2600 at some fantastic contract! *A bottom is a bottom.*

A vulnerable game, at duplicate, is worth exactly 500 points plus the trick score. The total value is from 600 points up to about 680 points. A sacrifice of 500 points against such a game is a paying sacrifice. A sacrifice of 700 points is a *disaster*.

If you are considering a sacrifice, therefore, you must look carefully at the vulnerability of both sides. Simple arithmetic and your bridge experience will tell you these things about sacrifices:

Neither side vulnerable: You can afford to be set two tricks doubled if the opponents have a game. This costs you 300 points, which is less than the value of their game. You cannot afford to be set three tricks, for that would cost you 500 points.

Opponents vulnerable: You can afford to be set three tricks doubled if the opponents have a game. This costs you 500 points, which is less than the value of their game. You cannot afford to be set four tricks, for that would cost you 700 points.

Your side (only) vulnerable: You can afford to be set only one trick if the opponents have a game. This costs you 200 points, which is less than the value of their game. You cannot afford to be set two tricks, for that would cost you 500 points. Clearly, you can very seldom afford to make sacrifice bids when you are vulnerable against non-vulnerable opponents. How often can you be reasonably sure that you will be set only one trick? It is usually more sensible to save your energy for the defense in the hope that you can find a way to defeat the opponents at their non-vulnerable game.

Both sides vulnerable: You can afford to be set two tricks if the opponents have a game. This costs you 500 points, which is less than the value of their game. You cannot afford to be set three tricks, for that would cost you 800 points—more than the value of any game.

The value of a part score in duplicate bridge is exactly 50 points plus the trick score. Occasionally, a part score bid and made produces a score of less than 100 points; for example, one notrump bid and made is worth 90 points (50 for the part score bonus and 40 for the trick score). Usually, however, a part score is worth slightly more than 100 points; for example, two spades bid and made is worth 110 points and an overtrick will bring it up to 140 points. One notrump with an overtrick is worth 120 points.

The cost of a one-trick set is usually 100 points or less. If you're not vulnerable, the defeat will cost you either 50 or 100 points. If you're vulnerable and the opponents fail to double, the defeat will amount to 100 points. A loss of 50 or 100 points is less expensive than allowing the opponents to score 110 points or 140 points for their part score contract. The difference between 100 points and 110 points is meaningless in rubber bridge, but in duplicate it may mean a difference of 5 or 6 match points.

YOUR TRUE OPPONENTS

Let us suppose that you begin a session of duplicate by sitting down in the East-West seats at Table 3. The North-South players at that table happen to be Mr. and Mrs. John Doe. You play as hard as you can against the Does, since they are your opponents. From another, and equally important point of view, the Does are not your *true* opponents. Your true opponents are all the other East-West pairs who will bid and play the very same cards that *you* are now bidding and playing.

The number of match points you will eventually get on any board depends on how well your score compares with the scores of all the other East-West pairs. If all the other East-West pairs bid the hand *very* foolishly, you can get a good match-point score for being only *slightly* foolish. If all the other East-West pairs bid and play the hand with great brilliance, you will get no match points at all for being just moderately clever.

It stands to reason that it will usually pay you to do very well against your flesh-and-blood opponents at the table. If you double them and set them 800, for example, that score of plus 800 for you will probably beat all the other East-West scores on that board. Nevertheless, you don't always try to collect the maximum against your flesh-and-blood opponents for reasons that have to do with your *true* opponents. This mysterious statement is best explained by the hand on the next page.

This bidding is not necessarily recommended, but it isn't particularly unlikely. East-West can actually make a game at hearts, losing only two clubs and one heart. South tries a sacrifice at four spades, and now West must double since there isn't the slightest chance to make *five* hearts.

West opens the king of diamonds, and East plays the queen as a signal. West obeys the signal by leading a low diamond at the second trick, and East wins with the ten. East now leads his

North
♠ 7 6 4 2
♥ K J
♦ 6 2
♣ A K Q 10 7

West
♠ A Q
♥ A 7 6 2
♦ A K 9 7 4
♣ 8 2

East
♠ 5
♥ Q 10 9 8 4
♦ Q J 10
♣ 9 6 5 4

South
♠ K J 10 9 8 3
♥ 5 3
♦ 8 5 3
♣ J 3

The bidding:

North	East	South	West
1 ♣	Pass	1 ♠	Double
2 ♠	3 ♥	3 ♠	4 ♥
4 ♠	Pass	Pass	Double
Pass	Pass	Pass	

singleton trump, South finesses the jack, and West wins with the queen.

At this moment West is at the crossroads. He must decide whether to lead a low heart in the hope that South will make the mistake of finessing dummy's jack—or whether to take the ace of hearts to make sure of getting a heart trick. West's decision will depend partly on vulnerability and partly on what he thinks is likely to happen when this hand is played at other tables. West's decision does not depend on what he thinks the actual declarer will do. West won't actually find out what happened on this hand at other tables until the entire session is over; during the game he can only *surmise* what other players are likely to do with the cards.

West has already taken three tricks, and he is sure of another trump trick. The question is whether to make sure of a fifth trick by taking the ace of hearts or to try for a sixth trick by leading a *low* heart.

West must think of what all the other East-West pairs will score with the same cards. If the other East-West pairs play the hand at two or three hearts, they will make 170 points. If the other East-West pairs play the hand at *four* hearts, however, they will make 420 points (or 620, if vulnerable).

West can surely set the contract two tricks by cashing the ace of hearts and taking the ace of spades at leisure. The penalty will be 300 points (or 500 N-S vul.), which is more than enough to compensate West for the loss of a part score. Hence West must cash the ace of hearts at once if he thinks that the other East-West pairs will stop at a part score.

If West thinks that most of the other East-West pairs will get to *four* hearts, he must try to collect a big enough penalty to make up for it. With neither side vulnerable, West may try for six tricks by underleading his ace of hearts. This is the play that will get West 100 or 500 points, depending on how South guesses the heart finesse.

If both sides are vulnerable, West surely should underlead the ace of hearts. This play gives him either 200 or 800 points. The larger penalty is enough to beat all the East-West pairs that bid and make a game; the smaller penalty is enough to beat all the East-West part scores. West could settle for 500 points by taking the ace of hearts, but it is very likely that he will get the same number of match points for either 200 or 500 points. Either score is better than a part score but not as good as a game. West can afford to ignore the play for 500 points and should concentrate on the play that gives him a chance for 800.

If North-South are vulnerable and East-West are not, West must surely cash the ace of hearts. This assures a penalty of 500 points, better than any East-West game. There is no advantage in collecting 800 points, since 500 points will probably be good enough for top on the board. When you have a pretty sure top, it's foolish to take any risks with it. You can't get better than a top, but you certainly can get worse.

If East-West are vulnerable, and North-South are not, West must surely cash the ace of hearts. There is no point in trying for 500 points since 500 and 300 points are both less than the East-West game but more than the East-West part score. West cannot possibly get enough to make up for the loss of his vulnerable game, but he can make sure of getting 300 points to make up for the loss of his part score. If he took a chance and wound up with only 100 points, he would be virtually sure of a bottom. All the other East-West pairs will surely get at least 140 points for a part score.

Few hands are as complicated as this, of course, but the underlying principles must become part of your match point philosophy. You must always keep in the back of your mind that other players are going to bid and play the same cards. Your score is in competition with the scores of those other players. This is the most important single principle in duplicate bridge.

WHAT IS THE FIELD DOING?

We have already seen that you sometimes ask yourself what the other players will do with your cards. This is true in the bidding as well as in the play of the cards.

Let us suppose that you must decide whether to stop at three spades or to go on to four spades. You think that the contract is fairly safe at three spades, but fairly risky at four spades. At rubber bridge you would bid four spades and take your chances. What should you do at duplicate?

You should bid four spades if you think that most of the other pairs will bid four spades on your cards. You should stay below game if you think that most of the other pairs will stop at a part score.

If you are in the same contract as the rest of the *field* you will have company whether the hand is lucky or unlucky. Hence you will get several match points even if you have made the wrong decision; and you may get a point or two above average if the decision turns out to be right.

If you act *against* the field, you will get a very good score when you are right, but you will get a very bad score when you are wrong. This is called *playing for top or bottom*.

Let's take another situation. You have decided to bid a slam, but you are wondering whether to go all the way to seven or stop at six. The decision should depend more on the field than on the nature of your cards!

In the average club duplicate, you are assured of better than average score on a board if you merely reach a small slam that can be made. There are always two or three pairs who fail to bid the slam, and your score surely beats theirs. If you bid a grand slam and go down, you are practically sure of earning yourself a cold bottom.

Let's compare gain with loss. Assume that you are playing in an 11-table game, so that 10 points is top on a board. If you content yourself with a small slam, you expect to get about 7 match points, perhaps more. If you bid the grand slam, you will get either 10 points or 0. Hence you are risking 7 or 8 points to pick up 2 or 3 points when you bid the grand slam. This doesn't pay unless the grand slam is very nearly a sure thing.

Take the same situation in a very *good* tournament. The small slam is so easy to bid that you judge that practically nobody will miss it. Moreover, you think that several pairs will bid the grand slam. The competition is so much stronger that you cannot sit back and collect a surely good score with a small slam. With a 10-point top, the match point result would probably be something like this:

3 or 4 points for stopping at six } if seven can be made
about 9 points for bidding seven }

7 or 8 points for stopping at six } if seven cannot be made
about 1 point for bidding seven }

You stand to gain about 4 or 5 match points by bidding seven, and you risk losing about 3 points. You can afford to bid this grand slam on an even-money chance. This, in fact, is a general principle of duplicate play: Don't bid a grand slam in a weak field unless it's practically a cinch; but bid a grand slam in a strong field if it seems fairly biddable and if you expect to have a *good* (not sure) play for it.

THE MINOR SUITS ARE FOR THE BIRDS

In rubber bridge the minor suits are respected members of the community. In duplicate bridge, the minor suits are social outcasts. You call on them only as a last resort.

Sometimes you won't have any choice. The only fitting suit in the partnership hands may be a minor suit, and notrump may be out of the question because of a singleton or a void or because one or two suits are wide open. Let's ignore these hands for the moment and turn our attention to the hands that can be played either at a minor suit or in some *other* contract.

If you can make only about one diamond or one club, you won't be playing the hand. You'll be defending against the opponents.

If you can make two diamonds (or clubs), you can score 90 points. If some other contract is possible, however, you may be able to bring in two of a *major,* worth 110 points. This is *very* much better because 110 will not only beat all those pairs who make only 90 points but it will also beat those who collected 100 points in penalties from their opponents. The step from 90 points to 110 is a big and important one. If you play this hand at notrump, you can probably make seven tricks for the same 90 points; and if you can steal an overtrick, you get 120 points—which is not only more than 100 but also more than 110.

On a hand of this sort, the traveling scoreslip will eventually show a variety of scores—some at 90, some at 100, some at 110, and so on. If you consistently play such hands in the minor suits you will usually make your contract, but you will wind up with very few match points. If you consistently play such hands at a major suit or at notrump, you will occasionally be set, but you will wind up with more match points in the long run.

If the hand is good enough to produce 9 tricks at a minor suit, it will be worth 110 points on the scoreslip. Such a hand may easily produce 8 tricks at notrump—worth 120 points. If notrump is out of the question, perhaps it will play at a major and produce 8 sure tricks with a play for a ninth. This gives you either the same 110 points or a chance for 140. Once again, you are better off abandoning the minor suit.

When you get to hands that will produce 10 tricks at a minor suit, you are getting near the game range. Many such hands will produce game at notrump, which is clearly worth more than four of a minor. If notrump is out of the question, perhaps the hand will be good for three of a major, which is worth 140 points while four of a minor is worth only 130 points. (If major suit and notrump are equally out of the question, this is one of the no-choice hands.)

When a hand will make game at a minor suit, it will make game at notrump surprisingly often. Even if one suit is wide open, perhaps the opponents won't lead it; or perhaps the opponents can take only four tricks even if they do lead their best suit. Five of a minor is worth only 400 or 600 points (depending on vulnerability); three notrump will give you the same result. One overtrick at three notrump will give you 30 extra points, which is better than one overtrick at five of the minor. What's more, it's far easier to make one overtrick at three notrump than at five of a minor.

For all of these reasons, tournament experts don't take the minor suits too seriously. At the low levels, a minor suit may be bid to show the strength of a hand without being treated as a true suit. At the high levels, insistence on a minor suit usually indicates some interest in a slam. After all, if the bidder is willing to play for 11 tricks in his minor suit, he can't be very far from a willingness to consider 12 tricks.

When you play rubber bridge again (most bridge fans play both games), remember to restore the minor suits to their proper status. This is one of the important distinctions between the two games, affecting opening bids, responses, and rebids.

NOTRUMP IS TOP DOG

Many hands will produce the same number of tricks whether played at a trump suit or at notrump. It pays to play such hands at notrump since that gives you the highest score. We have already seen that notrump is better than a minor suit; but remember also that it counts 10 points more than a major suit.

Remember also, however, that most hands will produce at least one trick more at a good fitting suit than at notrump. The score for four spades is 120 points; for three notrump, only 100 points. The major suit is worth 20 points more than notrump if it produces one extra trick.

There shouldn't be much question about your choice when you have a singleton or a void in either hand. The major suit will surely be better than notrump.

When both hands are balanced (no singleton or void), the presence of a weak doubleton should sway you. Such hands will usually play one trick better at a fitting major suit. If the doubleton is *strong,* however, there's no need to avoid notrump. When both hands have 4-3-3-3 distribution, notrump is surely the right spot for the hand.

At the slam range you must always consider the possibility of playing at six notrump rather than six of your best suit. If you can locate enough top cards during the bidding, you may be able to tell that the play for six notrump is as good as the play for six of the suit. The score is 10 points more than for six of a major. This is a very big difference in a good field, where many pairs can be expected to reach some slam contract. The 10 points will make little difference if the slam is very difficult to bid or if the field is weak; and then it is unwise to bid the slam in notrump if it is less safe than the slam at a suit.

Even at rubber bridge, certain slams are safest at notrump. Not only is there no danger of a ruff, but also you are not necessarily dependent on a reasonable break in a particular suit. If your trump suit breaks badly, for example, the slam usually goes down; but if you play the hand at notrump you may be able to recover by making enough tricks in the other suits.

COMPETITION IS THE LIFE OF DUPLICATE

When the opponents can make a game or a slam, there is no need for your side to bid. Many experts make it a practice to stay completely out of the auction in such situations. Some believe in making "interference bids." We'll eventually discuss both practices.

When the opponents can make only a part score, there's an excellent chance that your side can likewise make *something*. Perhaps you can't make as many tricks as the opponents, but it may pay you to bid for a one-trick set; or perhaps you can "steal" the hand from the opponents.

If the opponents bid one notrump or two of a suit and just barely make their contract, you will usually get very few match points on that board. This observation doesn't apply if the opponents have stumbled into a bad contract. Certainly, if you have five good trumps you'll let the opponents stew in their own juice rather than give them a chance to find a better contract. But if the opponents play the hand at a reasonable contract of one or two and just barely make their contract, you are headed for a bad score.

In such situations you have very little to lose if you make a competitive bid of some kind. Perhaps you will get a complete bottom instead of 1 or 2 match points, but what of it? Your bid may, instead, drive the opponents one trick higher; or it may cost you less than the enemy's part score, even if you are set. It will sometimes raise your score to 5 or 6 match points, and may even earn you a near-top. Despite the occasional bottom that you will surely get with such tactics, you will earn more match points in the long run.

You must therefore adopt two principles as part of your duplicate bridge philosophy:

1. When the opponents stop short at a low part score, you or your partner must get into the auction even with a rather poor hand. This general rule may be broken when you have length in the enemy's trump suit and when the opponents have bid as many as three suits. In the first case you have a chance to do well on defense; in the second, you may have no suit worth playing.

2. When your partner comes to life suddenly after the opponents have stopped short at a part score, remember that he may have bid with a rather poor hand. (See the first rule, above.) If he has a poor hand, you will have a good hand. After all, the strength must be *somewhere*, and the opponents have indicated that they don't have it all. In short, your partner has relied on the strength of your hand for his bid even though you have never done anything but pass. Don't make any further aggressive bids or doubles on the strength of your partner's bid. Be satisfied to play the hand at a part score or to have pushed the enemy one trick higher.

WHOSE HAND IS IT?

When both sides are in the auction, it is vital to know which side the hand really belongs to. Will the other pairs who hold your cards wind up with a plus score (for making a contract or for setting the opponents) or with a minus score (for going down or for allowing the enemy to make a contract)?

If the hand clearly belongs to the enemy, it doesn't pay to compete very hard. If you push too hard you may get doubled and set for more than the value of the enemy's part score or game.

If the hand clearly belongs to your side, be alert for a chance to double vulnerable opponents. You may easily collect more than the value of your part score or game.

If the hand doesn't clearly belong to either side, you are up against one of the most difficult problems in tournament play. If the opponents are hair-trigger doublers, you must bid cautiously, particularly when you are vulnerable. If the opponents are timid about doubling, you can afford to step out a bit more. You can be more adventurous when non-vulnerable than when vulnerable. All of the pairs who hold your cards will have much the same problem, after all, and when in doubt you should do whatever you think most of the field will do with your cards. Right or wrong you will have company.

If you are convinced that the hand belongs to your side, don't let the opponents steal it cheaply. Suppose you can make about three spades, and they have bid four diamonds. You have to double.

If the opponents make their doubled contract, you have lost very little. You would have earned very few match points for letting the enemy make 130 points at four diamonds. If you beat them one trick vulnerable, you get 200 points, more than the value of your part score. If the opponents are non-vulnerable, you probably have to hope for a two-trick set (300 points) to earn any match points; and this may come to pass. The important thing is not to let the opponents get away without a double. If you become known as a timid doubler, your opponents will be out stealing on every hand.

FATAL NUMBERS

You don't have to be an expert to know that it's fatal to be doubled and suffer some such fantastic penalty as 2600 points. Certain other penalties may look very innocent, but they're just about as dangerous.

For example, it's almost invariably fatal to be set 700 or 800 points. If the other pairs who hold your cards have a *game* bid and made against them, they will lose less than 700 points. Your score will beat only those pairs who have a *slam* bid and made against them. There will usually be very few such pairs because in the first place the slam may not be makable; and, second, only a few pairs may bid the slam even if it is an absolute laydown.

For the same reason it is usually fatal to be set 500 points when your opponents are non-vulnerable. Most of the players who hold your cards will be losing only 450 points or thereabouts.

The most common of all fatal numbers is minus 200. You achieve this delightful result when you are doubled and set one trick vulnerable. To lose 200 points is worse, of course, than to allow the enemy to bid and make a part score. You will therefore lose to all the pairs that held your cards and sold out at a low level. You will also lose to any pairs who bid just what you did but who were lucky enough to escape a double. You can get a decent match point score for your minus 200 only if the opponents have a game that is bid and made at *most* of the other tables. This sometimes happens, to be sure, but it is rare.

Curiously enough, a score of minus 300 is not quite so likely to be fatal as a score of minus only 200. When you are set *two* tricks, you usually know that you are sacrificing, and you probably *expect* to be set two tricks. You're not likely to do this except when the opponents have a game, when it pays you to sacrifice. In short, a score of minus 300 occurs when you know that the hand belongs to the enemy; but a score of minus 200 often occurs when it isn't clear whose hand it is.

Minus 150 is a somewhat rare bad score. If your opponents score 150 points for making 9 tricks at a notrump part score or 11 tricks at a minor suit part score, you have the consolation of hoping that game will be bid and made at the other tables. If you have dropped a trick in the play, however, you must expect a poor score. Moreover, if game is very hard to bid, you may get a poor score simply because your opponents are in notrump, making 150, instead of in a suit contract, making only 140 or 130 points.

Occasionally you will lose 150 points when you play the hand yourself. It's unusual to be set three tricks undoubled (non-vulnerable), but it's possible. If you have any choice in the play of the cards, you must do your best to hold the loss to minus 100 points. Presumably some of the other pairs who play your cards will be minus 110 or 140 when their opponents play the hand at a part score. Moreover, somebody else may be minus 100 points at your contract. Hence you will probably get a few match points for being minus 100, but you will get practically nothing for being minus 150.

It is usually fatal to let the opponents make any doubled contract. This sort of fatality happens to good players far more often than to beginners. As we shall see, the expert often doubles for a one-trick set. Some few of these doubles are bound to go wrong. The expert doesn't enjoy such an experience, but he endures it stoically as part of the price of expertdom.

HAIR-TRIGGER DOUBLES

In a rubber bridge game you seldom double the opponents unless you expect to beat them at least two tricks. You observe this rule not out of love or charity, but merely out of caution. A double that goes sour is expensive, and you must expect occasional expensive results if you double for a one-trick set. Hence, in rubber bridge, you wait until you can count on a two-trick set, knowing that you will still make a profit even if one of your tricks evaporates.

Likewise, you seldom double in rubber bridge unless you have a trump trick. A sure trump trick gives you some control, and also gives you the assurance that you aren't running into a freakish nine-card trump suit or the like.

These rules are very good for rubber bridge. Stick to them. In a duplicate game, however, such rules are a luxury that the winning player cannot afford.

In a duplicate game your opponents will fight hard for the part score whenever the strength is fairly equally divided between the two partnerships. If the hand *belongs* to you, it is vital to collect the 110 or 140 points (or whatever) that other pairs will score on your cards. To collect only 50 or 100 points may give you just as bad a score as though you had collected nothing at all; you will beat only those pairs who were actually *minus* with your cards instead of being plus.

The only chance you have to get a reasonable number of match points is to double the opponents whenever they outbid you on a hand that really belongs to your side. This will sometimes give you 200 or 300 points in place of your part score, and such a result will usually give you top on the board, or nearly a top. Even if the double gives you only 100 points, you may still gain a match point or two by beating some timid pair that failed to double and therefore collected only 50 points.

If the opponents make their doubled contract, as they sometimes will, waste no tears. It's true that you will have an absolute zero (although even that isn't invariably the case), but you have lost very little, since you were headed for a bad score in any case.

However, it isn't necessary to double the opponents when the hand belongs to *their* side. You will get a good score for *any* plus result, big or little. A double can never give you more than a top score, but it may give you less.

Take, for instance, the classic example of the expert who refused to double a grand slam with the ace of trumps in his hand! Strangely enough, he was one hundred percent right. He got top on the board for being plus 100, so he couldn't have earned any more match points even if he had doubled. His partner had been bidding spades with great determination and might have sacrificed at seven spades if he had been given one more chance to bid. A double would have given the partner one more chance, and the expert decided not to take any such risk.

This is an extreme case, to be sure, but the same principle holds true whenever the opponents voluntarily bid a game or slam that you are pretty sure to defeat. At the other tables, presumably, the bidding will be more sensible, and the players who have your cards will wind up with a minus score. Hence you are sure to get a good score even if you refrain from doubling. The disadvantage of doubling is that you may warn the opponents of danger and either drive them into a better contract or steer them to their best line of play.

WHEN TO JUMP OUT OF THE FRYING PAN

As we have several times observed, it pays to act vigorously in a duplicate game when you are threatened with a bad score on a particular board. Let's examine this principle a little more carefully, to show how it applies only to duplicate bridge and not to rubber bridge.

Suppose you bid up to three hearts in a rubber bridge game and the opponents then bid three spades. You *think* that you can beat three spades, and you feel pretty sure that you can't make four hearts. What do you do?

You pass. You're sorry to lose your chance to score 90 points below the line, but you're willing enough to accept 50 or 100 points above the line. If you double, the opponents may make their contract and thus score a game; and your double will then cost you about 500 points. You don't risk the loss of 500 points just to try for an additional 50 or 100 points. That is, you don't risk that sort of loss when there seems to be an even chance that the opponents will make their contract.

Simple arithmetic will show you why. If you double ten contracts of this kind, you will probably defeat five of them. You will gain 50 or 100 points on each of those five hands, so that your total gain will be about 350 points. But the enemy will *make* five of the hands, and you will lose about 500 points on each such hand. The total loss will thus be 2500 points. The net result of all ten hands will be a loss of more than 2000 points. Therefore such doubles are very unsound at rubber bridge.

Now let's take the same situation in duplicate bridge. Let's suppose that you can expect to get about 2 match points if you pass and let the opponents play the hand at three spades undoubled. If you double them and they make their contract, you get a cold zero. If you double and beat them, you average about 7 points per board. (This, by the way, is a quite reasonable estimate of how such a board will usually turn out.)

What happens if you pass on all such hands? You get 2 match points on ten such hands, for a total of 20 match points on the ten hands.

What happens if you double all hands of this sort? You get five cold zeros and five scores of 7 points. The total for the ten boards is 35 match points.

As you can see, the *exact* gain depends on several factors

that vary from one game to another. In the example given, the gain is 15 match points. In some duplicate games, the gain might run as high as 60 or 70 match points in a series of ten boards. It would seldom run below 15 points if your side could really make three hearts to begin with. If your side cannot make a part score, the hand really belongs to the opponents and there is no need for you to do anything unusual.

To sum up: The close double of a part score will land you in the poorhouse at rubber bridge but will boost your score substantially at duplicate.

We can formulate this as a general principle: Don't stay in the frying pan if there is a reasonable chance to land in safety. In a duplicate game, the fire isn't much hotter than the frying pan. To put it more concretely, almost *any* risk is worth while if you are surely headed for a bad score.

This principle must, however, be applied with a reasonable amount of common sense and caution. For example, suppose your opponents bid a slam and you must decide for or against a rather expensive sacrifice. The vulnerable slam, if made against you, will cost you 1430 points; the sacrifice will probably cost you 900 or perhaps even 1100 points. What should you do?

Let the opponents play their slam. If the slam is bid and made at most of the tables, you will get a few match points. If it is bid by practically nobody else, you will get a very bad score —whether you are minus 1430 or 900; in either case you will be beaten by all the pairs that didn't have the slam bid against them. There is no virtue in jumping from one frying pan to another. The only *real* hope is to pass and try to beat the slam.

PLAYING FOR AVERAGE

Most duplicate players go through several stages of development. As beginners they are timid and cautious. After they have gained some experience and knowledge, they often blossom out as wild men. And after some years in the wilderness they finally become steady and dependable experts.

The good bridge player is constantly tempted to do something unusual in the effort to get a top instead of a mere average score on the board. The expert resists most of these temptations.

There is a reason for this. The expert wants to win, but he isn't interested particularly in piling up the biggest score in history. He will win far more often if he tries for a comfortably good score than if he tries to set a record.

The expert knows that he will win almost any duplicate game (or perhaps land in second or third place) if he gets six or seven very good scores, provided that the rest of his scores are just about average. If he can't get many *very* good scores, he will achieve the same result with about ten *moderately* good scores, provided always that the rest of his scores are average.

The expert also knows that some of his opponents in the course of almost any duplicate game will step out of line in some way and practically beg to have their heads chopped off. The expert is obliging when it comes to such matters, and he gratefully accepts the match points that come along with the chopped-off head.

Hence the expert *plays for average* on every board—until an opponent makes a mistake. Only then does our expert try for a *very* good score on the board.

If the opponents make no mistakes, the expert contents himself with a *normal* result on the board. This will often give him above average on the board because some of the pairs who held his cards may have failed to achieve even the normal result. Sometimes, to be sure, the normal result is below average because mistakes were made at other tables, in which case other experts profited from them. In the long run, these tend to balance out. You get average scores from normal results; above-average scores when the opponents make mistakes; below-average scores when *your* side makes mistakes.

The ability to play for averages is partly a matter of temperament. Some players don't have the patience to wait for an opening. They want action on every board, even though this brings them many bad scores and sometimes makes them look rather foolish.

In a club duplicate, you can sometimes get away with playing for top or bottom on every board. Since this style tends to make a stooge out of your partner, you may have trouble finding partners once you become known as a wild man. In a championship tournament, the top or bottom style is actively discouraged by tournament officials since it tends to reduce the importance of skill and to increase the importance of luck.

Don't jump to the conclusion that playing for averages is unexciting. As we have seen, you must sometimes make risky doubles in the attempt to get a reasonable—average—score. And as we shall soon see, you must sometimes take other risks.

SAFETY ISN'T ENOUGH

You can't afford to bid and play timidly in a duplicate game. On part score hands you must do your share of bold bidding, for otherwise the opponents will steal most of them. On game-going hands, you must risk an occasional unsound notrump contract instead of a safe and sane game in a minor suit. Sometimes you must even choose a dangerous game in notrump rather than a safe game at a *major* suit.

The same principle holds true in the play of the cards. You can't afford to play all hands safe. You must often risk the contract in the attempt to make an extra trick.

It isn't always easy to decide when you must make the risky bid or the risky play. It is always tempting to adopt the conservative course, and sometimes it pays to do so.

Nevertheless, here is something to remember about duplicate bridge: The Lord hates a coward, and so does the official scorer.

Practically all of the successful tournament players are aggressive in the bidding and optimistic in the play. Even those experts who lean to the conservative side in close questions are firm and courageous once they have made up their minds that a particular risk must be faced. Nobody can win consistently at duplicate bridge if he tries to play cozy and safe.

Once you have recognized this fact, you will enjoy duplicate bridge more than ever. It exercises your intellect, your judgment, and your courage. No game can do more.

DUPLICATE ETHICS AND ETIQUETTE

When you play duplicate regularly, you will often sit across the table from an unfamiliar face. If that face wears a smile at the end of the evening, your evening is a success regardless of what the score may be. This statement is a bit on the stuffy side, but it is amazing and saddening that many veteran tournament and duplicate players get more enjoyment from badgering their partners than from any other feature of the game.

You also owe something to your opponents. They will occasionally surprise you by the silly things they bid or the odd way they find to play a hand. Write the score down blandly and wait until they have left the table before you discuss your brilliance or their lack of it. (If you are playing East-West, it is even easier to leave the table briefly at the end of the round and congratulate your partner at the watercooler.)

You will usually play two or more hands per round. Avoid discussing any of these hands with your partner or opponents until you have played the complete round. The player who spends minutes on post-mortems of the first hand and then has to rush through the second hand is one of the great plagues of tournament bridge.

Do not take it too much to heart when you get a very bad result on any board. The greatest players in the world still get bottoms every once in a while. Sometimes you can learn a lesson from your misfortune, and sometimes you can't. If it is just a miserable hand that your opponents have happened to guess right . . . call on the rueful smile that every bridge player must save up for just such occasions. It works much better than the sharp word or the furious glance.

When an irregularity of any kind takes place, sing out at once for the tournament director. The laws are always strictly applied in a duplicate game, even among friends, and only the director should state the law and announce the procedure or penalty. Never hesitate to invoke the laws and never resent it when the laws are invoked against you. Duplicate bridge becomes a hopeless muddle unless the laws are enforced invariably, uniformly, and impartially.

Try to make your bids and plays without hesitation and without showing either pleasure or displeasure. The idea is to get good results by the bid or by the play—not by the *manner* in which you bid and play. If your partner hesitates markedly over a bid or play, or if he clearly indicates his attitude towards a bid or a play, you must lean over backwards to avoid using the knowledge that you have thus illegally acquired. It isn't always easy to make all bids and plays equably, but there are few greater satisfactions than to be recognized as a very ethical player. (Curiously enough, "social" players are far worse offenders than experts, largely because they don't realize how wrong it is to convey their attitude or to profit from partner's mannerism.)

Be particularly careful to make all bids with the same language. Don't say "one spade" at some times and "I'll bid a spade" at other times. Always say "double" whether you are doubling for penalty or for takeout. (It is most reprehensible to say "double *one spade*" to make it clear to your partner that this is for takeout rather than for penalties.) Don't make some bids with gusto and others with a fearful quaver.

It's easy to go on with this list for paragraph after paragraph, but there is no need to belabor the point. Just don't seek any advantage that you wouldn't have if your partner were deaf, dumb, and blind. (Most partners *are,* of course, but that's another story.)

Try to cooperate with the tournament director in his effort to keep the game running smoothly. If he makes an announcement, listen to it. You may be able to correct the errors of those players who invariably talk all the way through all announcements.

3. Standard Principles of Bidding

Most duplicate players follow the standard principles of bidding, modifying them as necessary to fit them for duplicate instead of for rubber bridge. Before we go into the modifications, let's first review the standard outline of bidding.

THE POINT COUNT

Practically all experienced players use the 4-3-2-1 point count to determine the value of a hand. Older methods, which use honor tricks or quick tricks, are less accurate for the most part. Moreover, since most of the other duplicate players use the point count it will pay you to be familiar with it. You will want to discuss hands with other players, and you will therefore want to use the same language as your friends.

In valuing any hand, use the following count:

Each ace   = 4 points
Each king   = 3 points
Each queen = 2 points
Each jack   = 1 point

Since the value of a hand depends partly on its distribution as well as its high cards, you may count extra points for various long suits or short suits. There are two or three different ways of counting these points, and it doesn't matter very much which you use as long as you understand the underlying principle.

If you are planning to be the declarer, you may count extra points for *length* in the trump suit or in a usable side suit. Many players find it more convenient to count extra points for *shortness,* allowing 3 points for a void, 2 points for a singleton, and 1 point for a doubleton.

If you are planning to raise your partner's suit, you may count extra points for *length* in a strong side suit; and you may also count extra points for *shortness* in a side suit, provided that you have enough trump length to ruff your partner's cards in that short suit. When you have four or more trumps, your count for distribution may run fairly high. The easiest way to allow for this is to assume that game can be made with slightly less than the usual count when you have excellent trump support. Having made an adjustment of a point or two for this reason, you can count the same 3 points for a void, 2 points for a singleton, and 1 point for a doubleton.

If the bidding should make it clear that the partnership hands are a misfit, you must drop all distributional points except when your suit is absolutely solid. Thus, K-Q-J-10-9-8 is worth five tricks even if the hand is a misfit; but K-Q-J-5-3-2 may be worth only two or three tricks.

If you want to refine your count, you may add or subtract about 1 point because of the following reasons:

Add 1 point for all four aces.

Subtract 1 point from any aceless hand of 14 points or more.

Add 1 point to any strong hand after a bid by the right-hand opponent. Finesses will succeed for you.

Subtract 1 point from any strong hand after a bid by the left-hand opponent. Finesses will tend to lose.

Subtract 1 point if the hand contains one or more poorly guarded high cards. That is, take something off if you have a singleton king or a doubleton (or singleton) queen.

Add 1 point if the hand is exceptionally rich in tens and nines. They take tricks far more often than deuces and treys.

THE BASIC FIGURES

Most of your bids will indicate fairly clearly how many points you have. Likewise, most of your partner's bids will indicate *his* point count. After one or two bids, each of you should have a good idea of the combined total of points. When you have this total, you may guide yourself by the following basic figures:

HIGH CARD POINTS:

> Entire deck = 40 points
> Half of the strength = 20 points
> Game in a major or notrump = 26 points
> Small slam = 33 points
> Grand slam = 37 points

It pays to memorize these few figures. After you've used them a few times you'll find that it's no effort at all. You will then be ready to think of a few slight refinements.

Ordinarily, the hand belongs to the enemy when your side has 19 points or less. The opponents must have the balance of the 40 points in the deck, and they must therefore have 21 points or more. This is one way to find out *whose hand it is.*

If you have a fine fit in a particular suit, you can usually win seven or eight tricks with less than 20 points. Or you may be able to win eight or nine tricks with about 20 to 22 points. The fit is worth a point or two. This may help you in the bidding of part score hands, but remember that the opponents have a similar advantage in *their* suit if they have a good fit there.

At the game level, you ordinarily need about 26 points for ten tricks in a major suit or nine tricks in notrump. Reduce the count a point or so at notrump if you have a *strong* suit of five or six cards. Reduce the count a point or so at a suit if you have a fine fit.

You need more than 26 points to make eleven tricks. If you

must play the hand in a minor suit, don't go to game without about 28 or 29 points. Even then, give a last lingering thought to the possibility of playing the hand in notrump instead of the minor suit.

A small slam usually requires about 33 of the 40 points. This leaves 7 points for the enemy. If the enemy have precisely an ace and a king, they may defeat the slam. Usually they have something like a couple of queens and a king—or less. Although 33 is your basic minimum count for a slam, there's no law against having 34 or 35 points instead of the bare 33.

A slam may be made with less than 33 points when you have two very strong suits in the combined hands to provide the bulk of the tricks. You also need enough aces and kings (or voids and singletons) to prevent the enemy from making the first two tricks.

OPENING BIDS

One of a suit = 14 points to 23 points.

Two of a suit = 23 points or more, with unbalanced distribution.

One notrump = 16 to 18 points, balanced distribution, and stoppers in at least three suits.

Two notrump = 22 to 24 points, balanced distribution, and stoppers in all four suits.

Three notrump = 25 to 27 points, balanced distribution, and stoppers in all four suits.

One-and-a-half notrump = 19 to 21 points, balanced distribution, and stoppers in at least three suits. Show this sort of hand by opening with one of a suit and jumping in notrump at your next turn.

Three of a suit = A seven-card suit with 5 or 6 taking tricks not-vulnerable or with 6 or 7 playing tricks vulnerable. Substantially less than an opening bid in high cards.

Four of a suit = About the same as a three-bid, but one trick stronger.

RESPONDING TO ONE OF A SUIT

One-over-one* = a four-card or longer suit with a count of 6 to 17 points.

One notrump = 6 to 9 points. However, a response of one no-trump to one *club* shows 9 to 11 points. With less than 9 points, the responder can always find some cheaper bid.

Two-over-one* = a four-card or (usually) longer suit with a count of 10 to 17 points.

Two notrump = 13 to 15 points, balanced distribution, and the three unbid suits stopped.

Three notrump = 16 or 17 points, balanced distribution, and the three unbid suits stopped.

Raise to 2 = 6 to 10 points with Q-x-x or better in the trump suit.

Raise to 2½ = 10 to 12 points with Q-x-x or better in the trump suit. This bid is made by showing a side suit first and raising partner's suit next.

Raise to 3 = 13 to 17 points, with Q-x-x-x or better in the trump suit.

Raise to 4 = five trumps, a singleton or void suit, and at most 9 points in high cards. Usually a total count of 10 or 11 points.

Jump in new suit = 17 or more points, with either strong support for partner's suit or a very strong suit of one's own. With neither, the count should be at least 18 points.

Free bid or raise = substantially more than the minimum values for a response.

Pass = Fewer than 6 points. If the intervening player has bid, however, the responder may pass with as many as 9 points (if he has no convenient bid).

------

* A one-over-one is a bid in a higher suit than your partner's suit. He bids one of his suit, and you bid one of yours. A two-over-one is a non-jump bid in a suit that ranks lower than your partner's. He bids one of his suit, and you must bid two because your suit is lower.

REBIDS BY THE OPENING BIDDER

One notrump = minimum opening bid, balanced distribution.

Two of original suit = minimum or near-minimum opening bid, rebiddable suit.

One of new suit = 14 to about 21 points, almost surely only four cards in the new suit. (With 22 or more points the opener makes a *jump* rebid, since this continuing one-over-one is not completely forcing.)

Two of new suit (non-jump) = biddable suit, almost surely more than a minimum opening bid.

Two of new suit (*reverse*)* = at least 17 points, usually more. Second suit probably only four-carder.

Jump bid in new suit = at least 19 points; forcing to game.

Jump bid in notrump = 19 to 21 points, balanced distribution, stoppers in all the unbid suits.

Double jump to 3 NT = 21 points with a five-card suit or other extra strength; or 22-24 points not quite suitable for an opening bid of 2 NT. All unbid suits stopped.

Three of new suit (non-jump) = at least 17 points, usually more. Forcing to game, since the responder has also shown strength by responding at the level of two.

Raise to 2 of responder's suit = Q-x-x or better (usually four cards) in partner's suit, with a total count of 15 to 17 points.

Raise to 3 of responder's suit = Q-x-x-x or better in partner's suit, with a total count of 17 to 19 points.

Raise to 4 of responder's suit = Q-x-x-x or better in partner's suit, unbalanced distribution, and a total count of 20 to 23

---

* A *reverse* bid is a player's second bid, made at the level of two or higher, in a suit that ranks higher than the player's first bid. It guarantees strength because it may easily force the bidding up to the level of three. E.g., you open with one heart and bid two spades at your next turn. This may force your partner to bid three hearts and should therefore be based on considerable strength.

points. (Responder should consider a slam with about 10 points.)

Three of original suit (after a raise) = 16 to 18 points. Opening bidder may count 1 point extra for each card over four in his trump suit after that suit has been raised.

Four of original suit (after a raise) = 19 to 23 points. Opening bidder may count 1 point extra for each card over four in his trump suit after that suit has been raised.

Two notrump (after a raise) = 16 to 18 points, balanced distribution, with a hand that was not quite suitable for an opening bid of 1 NT. Not forcing.

Three notrump (after a raise) = 19 to about 23 points, balanced distribution, with a hand that was not suitable for an opening bid in notrump. Responder may go back to the original suit if a major, but must pass if it was a minor. Responder may *not* make a slam try.

Three of new suit (after raise of original suit) = 16 to about 23 points. This bid is forcing, and the opener may be merely *trying* for a game or may have made up his mind to bid a game regardless of the response.

RESPONDER'S REBIDS

There is great variety in the responder's rebids because of the large number of situations that may be created by the opening bid, the response, and the opener's rebid. It is easy, however, to find a few general principles that show what the responder's various rebids ought to mean.

Ordinarily, the responder can show his strength by the number of times that he bids. His general schedule is:

  0 to 5 points = no response at all
  6 to 10 points = only one response
 10 to 13 points = two responses
 13 to 17 points = enough responses to reach game
 17 or more points = possible slam try or slam bid

For example, suppose you make your response with 6 to 10 points. The opening bidder now bids either one notrump or two of his original suit. No forcing situation exists, and you have made your one response. Unless you have a very unusual hand, you should now pass.

If the opening bidder has made a rebid in a new suit, you may be unable to pass even though you have only 6 to 10 points. For example, you may like the original suit better than the new suit, in which case you should take your partner back to his first suit. This is called a "preference" and shows no extra strength.

If the opening bidder makes a forcing bid, you must make a second response even though your hand is worth only one bid. The opener knows that he has made a forcing bid, and he will not rely on extra strength unless you take some sort of positive action.

If the opening bidder makes a highly invitational bid, you may decide to accept the invitation even though you have only 6 to 10 points. For example, if your partner makes a jump rebid in notrump, showing 19 to 21 points, you would carry on to game with 7 points or more; but you would pass with a bare 6 points.

The responder can show a hand that is worth two or more responses by a single bid. For example, a response at the level of two shows at least 10 points; or an immediate response of two notrump shows 13 to 15 points; and so on.

With any strong hand, the responder counts the opener's points as shown by the opening bid and the opener's rebid; he then adds his own points and judges whether the total is enough for game or slam. If the total falls somewhat short of slam, the responder may make exploratory bids in the attempt to find out whether or not the needed points are present.

RESPONDING TO NOTRUMP BIDS

An opening bid of one notrump shows 16 to 18 points. The responder should add his own points to those shown by the opening bid to find out whether the combined cards are good enough for only a part score, a game, or a slam.

The responder should expect a game when he has 10 points, for then the combined count is 26 to 28. Game is still likely when the responder has only 9 points; and it is possible when the responder has only 8 points. Game is unlikely when the responder has 7 points, since then the count is only 25 points at most. Game becomes more and more unlikely if the responder's hand is reduced further. When the responder has only about 4 points, it is possible that the hand belongs to the opponents and that the bid of one notrump cannot be fulfilled.

The responder should expect a slam when he has 17 points, since then the combined count is 33 to 35 points. He should expect a grand slam when he has 21 points, for then the count is 37 to 39 points.

Most tournament players use some variation of the Stayman Convention for their exploration of game bidding after an opening bid of one notrump. A response of two clubs (the Stayman Convention) to one notrump asks the opening bidder to show a biddable major suit if he has one. This permits the partnership to bid game in a major suit, if a fit can be found; otherwise, in notrump. In some variations of the Stayman Convention, it is possible to explore part-score possibilities, but the primary purpose of the Convention is to reach a game contract.

In general, a response of two clubs, shows 8 or more points (usually more) and some interest in a major suit.

The opening bidder shows a major suit if he has only one; bids two spades first if he has biddable holdings in *both* majors; and bids two diamonds if he has no biddable major. (In some variations, the opener may bid two notrump without a major suit if he has an 18-point notrumper. Most tournament players avoid this bid.)

If the responder has a *long* major suit and a good hand, he need not bother with the Stayman Convention. Instead, he may jump to three of his suit in response to the opening bid of one notrump.

If the responder has no interest in a major suit but wants to get to game, he may raise notrump directly. He raises to 2 NT with 8 or 9 points; to 3 NT with 10 to 14 points. With 15 points or more, the responder should either consider a slam or make sure of one.

When the Stayman Convention is used, the responder may bid two spades, two hearts, or two diamonds, to show a weak hand that will play better in the suit than at notrump. The opener is expected to pass, since his strength has already been shown by the opening bid. If the opener has 18 points and a fine fit for the responder's suit, he may raise that suit to three as an invitation to game. The responder will consider this new evidence and decide whether or not the combined count is enough for game.

Any response to an opening bid of two notrump is forcing to game. The responder may pass with 0 to 3 points, but should bid with 4 points or more.

Any response to an opening bid of three notrump is a slam try.

DEFENSIVE OVERCALLS

A defensive overcall shows a strong trump suit of five cards or more. (On rare occasions, a four-card suit may be bid.) The bid is based not on points but on playing tricks, and the bidder should have enough trick-taking power to be safe against a prompt penalty double. This is sometimes expressed as being safe against a 500-point penalty.

To be safe within these limits means that an overcall at

the level of one guarantees at least 4 tricks, non-vulnerable; 5 tricks, vulnerable. An overcall at the level of two guarantees at least 5 tricks non-vulnerable; 6 tricks, vulnerable.

A jump defensive bid is used by most players to show a very strong hand. Such an overcall is not forcing but is highly invitational. Partner is invited to respond with slightly more than one sure winner. The jump overcall is used largely to show the first of two very strong suits or to show a one-suit hand of considerable strength.

A jump of more than one trick is used as a sort of shutout bid. The bidder shows a hand that is weak in high cards but reasonably safe against a penalty of 500 points. (Some players use the single jump overcall in the same way instead of using it to show a strong hand.)

An overcall of one notrump shows the same strength as an opening bid of one notrump.

THE TAKEOUT DOUBLE

A standard takeout double of an opponent's opening bid is made with about 14 points or more in high cards and either support for any other suit or a very strong suit of one's own. The double may be shaded down to about 12 points in high cards; and it may be made on as many as 20-odd points. When the hand is strong enough, an immediate bid in the opponent's suit is made instead of a takeout double.

South	West	North	East
1 ♥	2 ♥		

This sort of overcall (like a takeout double) *demands* a takeout and is forcing until game is reached. It follows that a takeout double shows a hand that at best was not quite good enough for an overcall in the enemy's suit, just as an opening bid of one in a suit shows a hand that was not good enough for an opening two-bid.

A minimum response to a takeout double shows 0 to 8 points. A jump response shows about 9 to 11 points and invites the doubler to continue to game if he has sound values for his double. If the double is a severe stretch to begin with, the jump bid may be dropped.

The doubler's partner can make *sure* of reaching a game by responding with a cue-bid in the enemy's suit:

South	West	North	East
1 ♥	Double	Pass	2 ♥

Such a bid does not guarantee any particular holding in hearts, but merely insists that the bidding be kept open until game is reached.

A response in notrump to a takeout double shows at least one stopper (usually more) in the enemy's suit.

A double of one notrump is primarily for penalties, not for takeout. Partner of the doubler bids with a long suit and a weak hand, but *passes with any strong hand*. The double shows about as much strength as the opening bid, so that the partner can pass if his own count indicates that the doubling side has more than 20 points in high cards.

A double of an opening three-bid is primarily for takeout, but the responder may let the double stand if he has balanced distribution and a smattering of defensive strength, such as three or more trumps and something like 7 points or more in high-card strength.

A double of an opening four-bid is primarily for penalties. An immediate bid of four notrump could be used instead of the double to demand a takeout. The doubler's partner may bid any long suit, however. The double will usually include support for most suits since it can very rarely be based on strength in the enemy's suit.

When the opening bid is passed by the responding hand, and also when the opening side drops the bidding at a very low level, the last player to speak may re-open the bidding with a takeout double. In rubber bridge such a double has no exact meaning except to indicate a desire to reopen the bidding.

The opening bidder may use a takeout double, likewise, to reopen the bidding:

South	West	North	East
1 ♥	1 ♠	Pass	Pass
Double			

This is a takeout double, showing substantial extra strength and support for any suit other than the enemy's suit.

A double is meant for penalties if the partner has previously bid or doubled. It is meant for takeout if the bid is one, two, or even three of a suit; if the doubler's partner has not previously bid or doubled; and if the double is made at the first opportunity to double. (Some of these distinctions break down in duplicate bridge.)

BIDDING OVER THE DOUBLE

When the opening bid is doubled for a takeout, the partner of the opening bidder should:

Redouble with any hand of 10 points or more.

Bid a reasonably sound suit with 9 points or less.

Raise the doubled suit as a shutout with shaded strength and trump support.

Pass any weak hand.

After such a bid or a redouble, the doubler's partner may pass to show weakness. If the doubler's partner bids, he shows some sort of reasonable suit and a count of about 6 points or more.

This chapter has been a summary of the standard bidding methods used by practically all good players at rubber bridge. In the next two chapters we will see how these methods are modified in duplicate bridge.

4. Offensive Bidding at Duplicate

Most bridge players follow the standard principles of bidding whether they are playing rubber bridge or duplicate. The most successful tournament players modify those principles slightly, however, to get winning results.

This chapter discusses the modifications that are necessary when your side is on the offense—doing all or most of the bidding—in duplicate bridge.

LIGHT OR STRONG OPENING?

Most successful rubber bridge players believe in opening the bidding whenever there is any excuse to do so. Some duplicate players likewise believe in light opening bids, but few of the great tournament players will open the bidding in first or second position with a doubtful hand.

There is a reason for this distinction. If you pass a doubtful hand in a duplicate game, and if the opponents open the bidding and then stop at a low level, you will be willing to take the risk of reopening the bidding at that time. In rubber bridge you will not be willing to take that risk later on, and you must therefore speak early or not at all.

For example, suppose you are the dealer and hold:

♠ J 6   ♥ K 10 7 6 3   ♦ 8 4   ♣ A K 5 4

In a rubber bridge game this would be an optional opening bid of one heart. In a duplicate game this is a good sound pass and no more.

The hand would be a proper opening bid in a duplicate game if it were improved to:

♠ J 6   ♥ K 10 7 6 3   ♦ K 4   ♣ A K 5 4

which has 14 points in high cards to make up for the weakness of the heart suit; or to

♠ 8 6   ♥ A K 10 7 6   ♦ 8 4   ♣ K J 5 4

which has a reasonably good heart suit, although it contains only 11 points in high cards, like the hand first shown.

Incidentally, it may be worth your while to compare the two hands a little more closely:

♠ J 6	♠ 8 6
♥ K 10 7 6 3	♥ A K 10 7 6
♦ 8 4	♦ 8 4
♣ A K 5 4	♣ K J 5 4

The second hand is a good deal stronger, even though both hands count to 11 points in high cards, with the same distribution. Not only does the second hand have a fairly strong heart suit in place of a rather moth-eaten suit, but also the black jack is better placed in the second hand. An isolated jack, especially in a short suit, has little value; but a jack accompanied by a higher honor has real value, especially in a long suit.

The trouble with making really light opening bids is that your partner must give you leeway *always*. He may understand perfectly well that your opening bid is quite sound about four times out of five—but he will *always* wonder whether this isn't the one mousetrap out of five. He will worry about doubling the opponents, or about stretching to try for game or slam, and he may well distort his bidding in order to make allowance for your supposed weakness. A tremendous amount of partnership trouble arises from this seemingly slight cause.

If you are expected to pass doubtful hands that count to 11 or 12 points in high cards, your partner must open fairly light in third or fourth position. If both of you passed such hands, you would sometimes pass with a combined count of 22 to 24 points, only to discover later that all the other pairs had bid and made a part score or even a game with the same cards.

Similarly, if you are going to pass doubtful hands in first or second position, your partnership must be willing to reopen the bidding on suspicion. If you pass to begin with and then stay out of the auction, your opponents will steal many of the hands in which the strength is fairly evenly divided.

If you cannot bring yourself to open the bidding light in third and fourth position, and if you cannot work up the courage to reopen the bidding when the opponents stop at a low level, then you cannot afford to pass a light hand in first or second position! It is better to take your chance with a doubtful opening bid than to let the opponents steal all of the close hands.

FOUR-CARD OR FIVE-CARD MAJORS?

It would be wonderful to have a five-card suit whenever you opened the bidding, in rubber bridge as well as in duplicate. Unfortunately there is no legitimate way to make sure that you are dealt a five-card suit in every hand.

You can get around this to some extent by bidding a minor suit of three or more cards whenever you have a biddable hand but lack a five-card (or longer) major. If you follow such a procedure, you will find yourself bidding three-card minor suits pretty often. This might bother you in rubber bridge, where the minor suits are not to be despised, but it won't bother you very much in a duplicate game, where the minor suits are comparatively unimportant.

Some tournament experts *never* open first or second hand with a four-card major suit. Many other experts *avoid* opening with a four-card major suit, but will make such a bid if there is no help for it.

A workable compromise is to open a hand with a four-card major only if it is exceptionally strong—A-Q-J-x or better. If the four-card major is any worse than that, open the hand with a three-card minor suit or with one notrump (if it measures up to notrump standards).

♠ J 8 6 5 3　♥ A Q 5　♦ K Q 6　♣ K 9

Bid one spade. The major suit is rather shabby, but it is a five-card suit and the hand is eminently biddable. Naturally, you would prefer to have more high cards in your suit rather than elsewhere, but there is such a thing as being *too* choosy.

♠ A Q 5 3　♥ K Q 7 5　♦ 7 6 4　♣ A 7

Bid one diamond if you have the courage of your convictions. (The orthodox bid is one spade, and this would be preferred in rubber bridge.) You bid a *three*-card minor suit when you have no suitable bid in a major. This hand probably belongs to your side, and you won't stay in a minor suit; you have merely made an approach shot. If the opponents unexpectedly outbid you, and if your partner must then make the opening lead, he will regard your diamond bid with suspicion. He knows that you showed a biddable *hand,* not necessarily a biddable *suit.*

♠ A K J 4　♥ K Q 7 5　♦ 7 6 4　♣ A 7

Bid one spade. This four-card major suit is biddable even though your partner may get the impression that you are bidding a *five*-card suit. You won't get very high in spades unless he has good support for the suit. You may get to about *two* spades with only three small spades in your partner's hand, but this won't bother you when you have good top command of the trump suit. It would be dangerous (in a duplicate game) to be in two spades with three small trumps in the dummy and a *mediocre* four-card holding in your own hand. This is the kind of contract that goes for a loss of 150 or 200 points.

♠ A K J 4　　♥ A 7　　♦ 7 6 4　　♣ K Q 7 5

Bid one club. There is never any reason to begin with the spades when you have biddable four-card holdings in both of the black suits. Always open with one club, since you are prepared to make a rebid of one spade over one diamond or one heart; and you are ready, likewise, to act over any other response you may get.

Let me repeat that it isn't *necessary* to guarantee a five-card suit when you open the bidding with a major. Many experts get good results without adopting this principle. If you feel more comfortable sticking to the orthodox bidding methods, do so, but even then, don't go out of your way to bid a four-card major; always make some *other* bid if you have a choice.

STEP-WISE BIDDING

In rubber bridge you can sometimes afford to play a hand in the "wrong spot," particularly when the difference is only 20 to 50 points or so. At duplicate you *must* aim for the right spot because everybody else may be there with your cards, and then you will have a bottom on the board. For this reason you always try to find a major suit in which both partners have four cards before you settle for a minor suit or even for notrump.

The easiest way to search for such a fit is to bid the cheaper suit whenever you have a choice of four-card suits at the level of one. For example, consider this sequence of partnership bids:

South	North
1 ♣	1 ♦
1 ♥	1 ♠
?	

The opening bid of one club shows a biddable hand but

not necessarily a biddable suit. South may have four cards in either major, or even four cards in *each* major.

The response of one diamond almost surely shows four or more diamonds. North would not bid one diamond with four diamonds and a *five*-card holding in spades or hearts, but he would surely bid one diamond with four or more diamonds and four cards in either major or even with four cards in *each* of the majors. For this reason, South does not give up the search for a major-suit fit; in fact, the search has just begun.

When South bids one heart, he shows a four-card suit. (Conceivably, South may have six clubs and five hearts, but this is unlikely. If it is so, South will make it clear later on. For the moment, it must be assumed that he is showing a four-card heart suit.)

If North had a four-card fit with hearts, he would raise at once. The search would be over. Even if North had a biddable spade holding, he wouldn't bid it—except as a temporizing bid, made with the intention of raising the hearts later on.

When North does bid spades, it must be assumed for the moment that he has a four-card holding in spades and that he does *not* fit the hearts. (If he does fit hearts, he will raise that suit later on, probably with a jump bid to make it quite clear that he had this well in mind all the time.) Apparently North has four or more diamonds and a four-card spade suit.

South is now in position to raise the spades if he has a four-card spade holding. Lacking such support for spades, South may make whatever bid his hand seems to call for. He may rebid clubs (if this is a real suit), raise diamonds, or bid some number of notrump.

Whatever happens from now on, this much is sure: If the partnership hands contain a 4-4 fit in a major suit, at least one of the partners will be aware of it.

There are some important minor principles bound up with this. If a player skips over a suit, he doesn't have four cards in the suit he has skipped—or, conceivably, he has *five or more* cards in the suit he has bid. This sounds complicated, but a few examples will show that it's really very simple:

South	North
1 ♣	1 ♠

North cannot have four hearts *and* four spades, for with any such holding he would bid one heart instead of one spade. Hence North probably doesn't have four hearts. If he does have four hearts, he must have five or more spades.

South	North
1 ♣	1 ♠
2 ♣	2 ♥

North has at least five spades. He may also have a five-card heart suit. He cannot have two four-card suits, for then he would bid one heart instead of one spade.

Sometimes the knowledge of this principle stops you from bidding a suit that is quite biddable. You know that your partner will not have support for the suit, and there may be no advantage in giving information to the enemy. For example:

South	West	North	East
1 ♥	Pass	1 NT	Pass
?			

You, South, hold:

♠ A Q 9 5　　♥ A K 8 5 4　　♦ A 4　　♣ K 3

There is no need to bid the spades, since your partner cannot have any four-card holding in that suit. Raise to two or three notrump depending on how much leeway you allow your partner in this situation. If you say nothing about the spades, you may get a spade opening lead, which you can probably stand better than one of the minor suits. Your partner probably has length and some strength in *one* of the minors, but the other minor suit is probably the weak spot of the hand.

THIRD HAND BIDS

It pays to open the bidding somewhat light in third position (after two passes) because your partner may have been unwilling to open a doubtful hand as the dealer. It is possible that the hand belongs to your side even if neither one of you has a sound opening bid. Hence you tend to open with 10 points or more in high cards.

There is no value in overdoing this. If you open third hand with almost any assortment of garbage, your partner never knows whose hand it is and at what level. The bidding then degenerates into a guessing contest for your side.

The opponents are seldom puzzled in such situations. They can get good results by merely making their normal bids. If you, their opponents, step far out of line, they will punish you. Occasionally, a psychic bid by third hand will talk the opponents out of a game or cause them to stop at game when they have a slam; but far more often a very weak third-hand bid will either fizzle completely or lure the bidder's partner into a dangerous error.

The most successful match point bidders open most 10-point hands in third position, and will open a 9-point hand if the bid can be used to indicate a desirable lead. They seldom go below 9 points, and they seldom pass 10 points. (The few experts who believe in very light opening bids in first position don't need to open 10-point hands in third position. They may comfortably wait for 11 or 12 points.)

One of the important reasons for passing a *weak* hand (less than 10 points) in third position is that the hand almost surely belongs to the enemy. You and your partner almost surely have fewer than 20 points in high cards, in which case the opponents must have more than 20 points. If the opponents have enough for a game, your hand will probably contain most of the strength that they are missing. Your bid will reveal that fact and help them in the play.

There is no need to insist on a five-card major for a bid in third or fourth position. It is safe to bid a four-card suit, provided that it isn't so weak that you prefer your partner to lead something else. In other words, you still need a fairly strong four-card suit, but you will settle for something like K-Q-J-x or even K-Q-x-x.

Test your third hand bids with the hands that follow. Assume in each case that you are third hand after two passes:

♠ K 9 7   ♥ K Q J 6 3   ♦ 8 5   ♣ 7 6 2

Bid one heart. You have only 9 points in high cards, and would prefer to have more for your third-hand bid. Nevertheless, it may be important to get your partner to lead a heart if he should eventually be the opening leader.

♠ 10 9 7   ♥ K Q J 6 3   ♦ 8 5   ♣ 7 6 2

Pass. It doesn't pay to open a 6-point hand in *any* position. Such a bid may occasionally produce a good result, but it will cost you more than it gains in the long run.

♠ K Q J   ♥ K 9 7 6 3   ♦ 8 5   ♣ 7 6 2

Pass. It doesn't pay to open a 9-point hand unless you can thereby suggest a desirable opening lead. In this case you have no reason to assume that a heart opening lead will be favorable to your side. Hence you pass *quickly*. (An opponent will probably be the declarer, and he might profit from guessing at your strength if you passed with obvious regret!)

♠ K Q J   ♥ K 9 7 6 3   ♦ 8 5   ♣ Q 7 6

Bid one heart. You practically always open with 11 points after two passes. Conceivably, your partner has passed a hand of about the same strength, in which case your side can make a part score—or even a game. You would prefer a stronger suit for your opening bid, but you can't afford to wait until a perfect hand comes along.

♠ K Q 6   ♥ K 9 7 6   ♦ 8 5   ♣ Q J 7 6

Bid one club. The 11-point hand is worth opening. As usual, with four hearts and four clubs, you open with a club bid.

♠ K Q J 6   ♥ K 9 7 6   ♦ 8 5   ♣ Q 7 6

Bid one spade. The 11-point hand is worth opening in third position, and the strong four-card major is the least of the evils.

When you open in third position with only 10 or 11 points in high cards, you have every reason to believe that your side has no game. You therefore intend to drop out of the bidding at the first convenient opportunity.

If your partner makes a jump response in a new suit, you will bid again. Game is not out of the question in this case. We'll discuss this subject more fully in a short time.

If your partner responds in your singleton, you bid again. Sometimes you find a second bid if your partner responds in your doubleton. If your doubleton is Q-x or better, you tend to pass.

If your partner (who has already passed) makes a non-jump response of a convenient nature, you simply pass. Further bidding would sound as though you were interested in game, and your partner might well wax too ambitious because of that impression.

One of the most important things to remember about third-hand bids is that they're often perfectly sound. No law says that you must have a weak hand simply because you're in third position. If you have a *sound* opening bid, you can afford to make a normal rebid instead of passing your partner's response.

For example, let's take one of the weak hands again:

♠ K Q 6   ♥ K 9 7 6   ♦ 8 5   ♣ Q J 7 6

You open with one club, intending to pass if your partner bids one spade, one heart, one notrump or two clubs (or even *three* clubs). You don't intend to pass one diamond, mostly because it's silly to open a hand and pass at one diamond, making your weakness clear to the enemy while it is still convenient for them to enter the auction.

Let's strengthen the hand slightly:

♠ K Q 6   ♥ A Q 7 6   ♦ 8 5   ♣ Q J 7 6

You now have a full opening bid, with 14 points in high cards. You still open with one club, but you intend to rebid. If your partner bids one heart, you will raise to two hearts. If he bids one spade, you will bid one notrump or two spades (a very close choice). If your partner bids one notrump, you will bid again because the response of one notrump to an opening bid of one club shows 9 to 11 points and balanced distribution. (It's not easy to find a convenient bid over one notrump, but that's another story. Two hearts or two notrump are probably the best bets.)

If you do rebid in any way that shows strength, your partner will understand that you have a legitimate opening bid or more. If he has about 10 points or slightly more, he can begin to think about trying for a game.

FOURTH HAND BIDS

Some good duplicate players practically never pass out a hand, no matter how weak it may be. They're afraid that other players who held their cards somehow managed to get a plus score and that they will get a poor match-point result for passing.

This view is too extreme. When your hand is very weak, the opponents can probably make a part score or can probably beat you at some low contract. If you open the hand, you will wind up with a *minus* score, whereas you can avoid the minus score by passing.

In deciding for or against a fourth-hand opening bid, you use almost but not quite the same principles as in third position. Bid with 11 points or more in high cards. Bid a 10-point hand with a good spade suit, or with good hearts and some length in spades. Pass almost any 9-point hand, unless it is fairly powerful in playing tricks. Pass any 10-point hand that lacks strength in the major suits.

These guiding rules may be varied somewhat to fit the partnership style. If your partner opens the bidding with a light hand, you are entitled to assume that he doesn't have 11 or 12 points in high cards when he passes. Hence you will pass 10 points cheerfully in fourth position, and you will tend to pass 11 points if the hand contains no strength in the majors. If, however, your partner tends to pass all doubtful hands, you know that he may well have up to 13 points even though he has passed. Hence you tend to open a 10-point hand and will surely open any 11-point hand.

The main principle is that you want to open the bidding if there is reason to hope that your side has more than half of the 40 points in the deck. If there is no reason to hope for 21 points or more in the combined hands, you are happy to pass the hand out.

BIDDING BY THE PASSED HAND

When you have passed originally, your partner knows that your strength is limited. Your ceiling is at 11 or 12 points in high cards, with an occasional 13-pointer. Your floor is as low as 0 points, although this is about as rare as the 13-point-pass.

If your partner opens the bidding in third or fourth position, you will want to indicate quickly and safely whether you are near the floor or near the ceiling. Your partner will then know whether the hand should be played at a part score, at a game, or at slam.

It would be simple if you could afford to make some sort of jump bid with 11 points or more in high cards, indicating a *maximum pass*. You can't always afford that, but a jump response is the best way to show your strength if the jump is convenient.

You avoid jumping to two notrump when your partner has

opened third hand. Few bidding situations are more annoying than an opening bid third hand with 9 or 10 points and a jump to two notrump by the passed hand with 11 points. The partnership is now in a dangerous contract, and the reproaches will fly thick and fast. One player will say "I can't afford to open the bidding light if you're going to leap around like that." The other will say, "I don't know what to do if you're going to open third hand with such dogmeat."

The solution is to make some other response, if possible, without committing yourself immediately. Bid a higher-ranking suit, if you have one; raise your partner's major suit if you have trump support. In a pinch, bid *one* notrump on the theory that *somebody* (partner or opponent) will make another bid. If you have passed a very good 12-point hand or the rare 13-pointer, and if no *convenient* bid is available, make the jump response of two notrump and take your chances.

You can afford to be a little less cautious when your partner has opened in *fourth* position. He may have a sub-standard opening bid, but it will not be *far* below standard. You can afford to jump to two notrump with a good 11 points or with 12 points, and the partnership will be on fairly safe ground.

The first rule of bidding by the passed hand is: *Don't get out of the major suit.*

For example, suppose that your partner opens in third position with one heart. If you have three or more hearts in your hand, avoid bidding a new suit. With a very bad hand and only three hearts, bid one notrump or pass. With a mediocre hand, bid two hearts. With a maximum pass, bid *three* hearts. Don't bid two clubs or two diamonds; and don't even bid one spade. The risk is too great that your partner will pass your response, and you will then be in a minor suit or in the wrong major.

It is all right to make a *jump* bid in a new suit, since that is forcing. You will have a chance to get back to the good major suit.

Let's take a few examples, with the following bidding for each:

South	West	North	East
Pass	Pass	1 ♥	Pass
?			

♠ K J 5 2 ♥ K 8 4 ♦ K 9 7 3 ♣ 6 2

Bid two hearts. This is a very meaty hand for a simple raise, and North should make allowance for this possibility if he has substantially more than a minimum opening bid. If North has a sub-standard opening bid, however, he will be grateful for your restraint. If you were not a passed hand, you would bid one spade.

♠ K J 5 2 ♥ 6 2 ♦ K 9 7 3 ♣ K 8 4

Bid one spade. This is the same hand, with some of the suits exchanged. Since you lack support for hearts, you can afford to show a suit of your own. Note that you didn't dream of showing the spades in the previous hand.

♠ K 8 4 ♥ 6 2 ♦ K 9 7 3 ♣ K J 5 2

Bid one notrump. Again, a very meaty hand for a very weak-sounding bid. North should take this possibility into account if he has extra strength. If he has a weak hand, you will be in the right spot. If he has a bare opening bid, of about 14 points in high cards, one notrump is a reasonable contract. Moreover, if one of the opponents reopens the bidding, you will double and should collect a handsome reward.

♠ 8 4 2 ♥ 6 2 ♦ A K J 9 7 ♣ Q 5 2

Bid two diamonds. This is a reasonable contract to stop at if North has a weak hand. If North has a sound opening bid, he will rebid, and you will probably get to game. For example, if North now bids two notrump, you will raise to three notrump. If North, instead, bids two hearts, you will bid two notrump.

♠ 8 4 2   ♥ 6   ♦ K Q J 9 7 3   ♣ Q 5 2

Bid two diamonds. You intend to bid three diamonds at your next turn, if possible. This sort of bidding by a passed hand suggests that your hand is good at diamonds but not good for much else. If you were not a passed hand, you would have an ugly choice between a response of one notrump (which conceals the distribution) and two diamonds (which exaggerates the strength). In rubber bridge, most experts would bid two diamonds; in duplicate, most experts would prefer one notrump. As a passed hand, however, you can afford to bid two diamonds without fearing that North will credit you with a very strong hand.

♠ 8 4 2   ♥ Q 5 2   ♦ A K J 9 7   ♣ 6 2

Bid three hearts. This is a slight overbid, but two hearts would be an even worse underbid. Since you are a passed hand and have good support for your partner's major suit, you must choose between the single and the double raise. If you were not a passed hand, you would bid two diamonds first and show your support for hearts at your next turn.

♠ 8 4 2   ♥ Q 6 5 2   ♦ A K J 9 7   ♣ 2

Bid three hearts. This is a very comfortable double raise. If North has a sub-standard hand and decides to pass, the result will be satisfactory. If he has a sound opening bid, he will probably go on to game, for which there should be a fair play.

♠ 8 4   ♥ Q 7 6 5 2   ♦ A K J 9 7   ♣ 2

Bid three diamonds. This jump shift by a passed hand is the equivalent of a jump to four hearts. If your partner has a sub-standard opening bid, you still want to be in four hearts. If he has a good hand, however, the bid of three diamonds will give him more information and will thus help him decide for or against a slam.

OPENING SHUTOUT BIDS

An opening bid of three or four in a suit is meant chiefly to shut the opponents out or to make it difficult for them to choose their best contract. In some ways you can be more venturesome with such bids in duplicate than in rubber bridge, but in other respects you must be more cautious.

The strength of your hand must be such that your opponents are unlikely to double and collect more than the value of their game (if they *have* a game). As you can see, your actual cards are only one of many factors. You must also consider the vulnerability of both sides, the caliber of the opponents, and the likelihood that the opponents have an easily biddable game.

For example, you need a very good hand to make a shutout bid when you are vulnerable against non-vulnerable opponents. If they double you and set you two tricks, they will score 500 points, which is more than the value of their game. Even if they double and set you only one trick, they will collect 200 points, which is more than the value of a part score.

As a practical matter, therefore, there is almost no such thing as a vulnerable shutout bid against non-vulnerable opponents. A hand good enough for such treatment is good enough for a normal opening bid.

At the other extreme, almost any seven-card suit is strong enough for a shutout bid when you are non-vulnerable against vulnerable opponents. They must double and beat you *four* tricks in order to get full value for their game. If they beat you only three tricks, collecting only 500 points, they may get a bottom on the board. If the opponents could only tell when to do so, they could often double a really ragged three-bid and set it four tricks, but they will seldom have the nerve to do so. More often, they will try to bid their game or slam in spite of the fact that your bid has robbed them of several levels of bidding.

When the vulnerability is equal, you must be within two tricks of your contract to be safe against a disastrous double.

Even here, however, you are reasonably safe if you have a good strong trump suit—such as K-Q-J-9-6-5-2. It is very unlikely that either opponent has enough trump strength to double you for penalties or to make a penalty pass of his partner's double. You have no such assurance, however, if your trump suit is something like K-J-8-6-5-4-3. It is far easier for an opponent to have the makings of two trump tricks, in which case he will work towards a penalty double if he can.

When you make a shutout bid, you take control of the bidding temporarily—sometimes permanently. Therefore, it isn't a sound tactic to make a bid of three clubs or three diamonds as dealer or second hand when you have three or more cards in a major suit. For all you know, your partner may have a very good hand, with length in that major suit. Your shutout bid will then stop a game, but it will be your partner's game rather than that of the enemy.

You needn't worry too much about three-card support for a major suit if you are making your shutout bid in the other major or if your partner has already passed. If you have a seven-card major suit, you aren't worried about the other major. If your partner has already passed, game should be out of the question for your side, and your shutout bid may work havoc with the enemy.

♠ Q 10 7 6 5 3 2   ♥ 8   ♦ 4 3   ♣ K J 4

Bid three spades if not vulnerable against vulnerable opponents, and whether you are first, second, or third hand. (If you were fourth hand, you would pass quickly and then try to find out who had passed an opening bid!) This hand may take only five tricks, but the opponents are not likely to find out; one of them will almost surely bid. With any other vulnerability, however, this hand would rate only a pass.

♠ Q 10 7 6 5 3 2   ♥ 8   ♦ K 3   ♣ K J 4

Do *not* bid three spades in any position or any vulnerability. A hand with strength in three suits is not proper material for pre-empting. In first or second position, you pass with this hand. In third or fourth position, you bid *one* spade and hope to buy the hand cheaply. Never underestimate the power of the spade suit in competitive hands.

♠ K J 4   ♥ 8   ♦ Q 10 7 6 5 3 2   ♣ 4 3

Bid three diamonds with this hand only if non-vulnerable against vulnerable opponents and only if third hand. The hand is too weak for a pre-empt (or anything else) with any other vulnerability. In first or second position you would avoid pre-empting when you have such good support for spades.

A shutout bid may work beautifully on a particular occasion and against particular opponents even if you break every rule known to experts. Some players have been known to open with a three-bid on a small doubleton! In the long run, however, you will get better results by sticking to the rules. What's more, you will avoid offending your partner with a control-taking bid when your hand doesn't call for taking control.

DELICATE FORCING BIDS

Certain bids are treated as forcing in duplicate bridge even though they aren't listed as forcing in any of the textbooks. Certain other bids are treated as nearly forcing. A successful duplicate player should be familiar with these situations.

Begin with this situation:

South	West	North	East
1 ♥	Pass	2 ♣	Pass
2 ♥			

North has shown about 10 points or more by his response at the level of two. Such a hand is almost always worth a second bid opposite an opening bid. If South can be depended upon to have a reasonably sound opening bid, the partnership values must be at least 24 points in high cards; and North cannot afford to pass. If, however, South is allowed to have a "mousetrap" as his opening bid, the partnership values may be only about 21 points in high cards, and North may worry about making a second bid.

In a good partnership, a response at the level of two almost guarantees a willingness to bid again. Hence the opening bidder can afford to make a minimum rebid (if his hand isn't good enough for more energetic action) without fearing that he will be prematurely dropped.

The position is even clearer with this bidding sequence:

South	West	North	East
1 ♥	Pass	2 ♣	Pass
2 ♦			

South hints strongly at extra values when he bids a new suit, although he doesn't actually *guarantee* more than a minimum opening bid. Since North should have at least 10 points, and South indicates more than a bare 13 or 14, a forcing situation exists. North shouldn't dream of passing.

Once every ten years or so, North will have a desperation response of two clubs such as:

♠ 7 6 3   ♥ – – –   ♦ J 9 5   ♣ K Q J 8 5 3 2

North was afraid to pass one heart and didn't want to bid one notrump with a void in one suit and seven cards in another. If North now wants to pass the rebid of two diamonds, he will probably be forgiven. Aside from such extreme and unlikely situations, however, the bidding sequence is considered forcing.

The force would be even stronger if South has reversed:

South	West	North	East
1 ♥	Pass	2 ♣	Pass
2 ♠			

South shows a probable 17 to 19 points by his reverse bid of two spades. North shows about 10 points by his response at the level of two. The partnership values are enough for game, so it is inconceivable that North will drop out at this early moment.

It is possible, of course, that South has shaded his values

for the reverse down to about 16 points because he relies on North to have a good hand for the two-over-one response. A good South would not shade below 16 points, and a good North would not shade below 9 points; so that the partnership values would still justify further bidding.

Not all reverses are forcing. For example:

South	West	North	East
1 ♥	Pass	1 NT	Pass
2 ♠			

South should have a full 17 to 19 points for this rebid of two spades. There is no excuse for shading in this situation, since North may have only 5 or 6 points. North may well pass if he has only such a minimum, but he will tend to find another bid if he has 7 or 8 points; and North will be delighted to bid again if he has his maximum value of about 9 points.

In many partnerships this particular sequence of bids is practically forcing even if North has minimum values. North is expected to respond with one spade instead of one notrump if he has any four-card holding whatever in spades—even 5-4-3-2. The response of one notrump therefore *denies* a four-card spade holding. Under these circumstances, why is South bidding a presumed four-card spade suit when he *knows* that his partner lacks support for the suit?

Conceivably, North may want to pass two spades with a bad hand that includes three spades and only a singleton heart. It is far more likely, however, that an expert South is gambling that North will not have the rare hand that calls for a pass, and that South doesn't have a real spade suit at all.

South may have such a hand as this:

♠ K 8   ♥ A K 7 5 3   ♦ A 10 5   ♣ A J 9

The orthodox bid is a raise to two notrump with this hand. A crafty South may bid two spades with the intention of bidding three notrump at his next turn—if he gets a next turn. If South gets away with this bid he will probably discourage a spade lead, and his partner should have an easier time at three notrump.

The opening bidder hints at extra strength whenever he shows a new suit, but he can't always rely on this hint to create a forcing situation. For example:

South	West	North	East
1 ♥	Pass	1 NT	Pass
2 ♦			

The rebid of two diamonds may be passed. North will naturally be reluctant to play the hand at a minor suit if there is any reason to hope for a good result at hearts or at notrump; but North will cheerfully accept diamonds if he has a singleton heart and a weak hand. North would pass two diamonds with:

♠ Q 7 4   ♥ 6   ♦ 7 5 3 2   ♣ K J 9 7 6

In this situation, South must make a stronger bid if he has a *very* good hand. Depending on the nature of his hand, he can raise notrump directly; or bid *three* diamonds; or make a jump rebid in hearts.

The fact that North is not *forced* to bid again should not prevent him from bidding voluntarily if there is any excuse to do so. North should automatically go back to hearts if he has any three cards in the suit. North should even go back to hearts with a good doubleton, such as Q-x or better. If South is known to have a five-card major suit, North should return to hearts with *any* doubleton.

North cannot go back to hearts with a singleton, but he should give some thought to a further bid if he has maximum values for his response of one notrump. He should raise to three diamonds if he has:

♠ Q 7 4   ♥ 6   ♦ K 5 3 2   ♣ K J 9 7 6

There may be a game in diamonds or notrump. If South has only a mediocre hand and therefore passes three diamonds, there should be a very good play for the contract. South can hardly expect to find a stronger dummy than this, in view of the response of one notrump, so the partnership should not get too high.

The situation is much the same when the first response is a one-over-one rather than one notrump:

South	West	North	East
1 ♥	Pass	1 ♠	Pass
2 ♦			

South's bid is not forcing, but it hints at extra strength. North will usually be able to find another bid, but South can't rely on this. If South has a *very* good hand, he should make a jump rebid of some kind.

If the responder has raised the first suit, a bid in a new suit is forcing:

South	West	North	East
1 ♥	Pass	2 ♥	Pass
3 ♦			

North is expected to bid again. If he can find nothing else to say, he must go back to hearts. It is inconceivable that South wants to play the hand at a minor suit after the heart suit has been bid and raised.

North would still be obliged to find another bid even if the bidding were:

South	West	North	East
1 ♥	Pass	2 ♥	Pass
2 ♠			

It is possible to construct a hand with which the partnership can make only two spades and nothing else. Such hands are, however, very rare. The partnership will come to no harm if North always finds another bid in such situations. If South can rely absolutely on this bid as a force, he can make it without a real spade suit if he wants to discourage a lead or pave the way for a notrump contract.

For example, South may have:

♠ K Q 8   ♥ A K J 9   ♦ Q J 10 6   ♣ 5 3

There is a chance for game in hearts or notrump if North has raised with maximum values. One rebid is as good as another if North has a maximum with four hearts, since North will gladly go to four hearts at his next turn. If North has only a three-card heart holding, however, notrump may be the best spot. An exploratory bid of two spades has the advantages of being cheap and informative at the same time. South cannot afford to make this delicate bid, however, unless he knows that North will treat it as forcing for one round.

The responder can do his share of delicate forcing by bidding a new suit at his second turn. For example:

South	West	North	East
1 ♦	Pass	1 ♠	Pass
2 ♦	Pass	2 ♥	

South must find another bid even if he has already shown his full values. Presumably, North will make allowance for the fact that he has held the pistol to his partner's head and forced him to bid.

In this situation, South would bid two spades with:

♠ 9 7 2   ♥ A 8   ♦ A K J 8 5 3   ♣ 6 4

This simple preference bid would not show more than three-card support. Lacking three-card support for spades, South would bid three diamonds with:

♠ A 8   ♥ 9 7 2   ♦ A K J 8 5 3   ♣ 6 4

South would avoid a real raise of the hearts with only three-card support. If North rebids the hearts, however, South will be happy to raise the suit.

South would not "sign off" in notrump without a stopper in the unbid suit. For example, he would not bid notrump with the worthless doubleton in clubs just shown. He would bid two notrump, however, if the hand is slightly changed:

♠ 6 4   ♥ 9 7 2   ♦ A K J 8 5 3   ♣ A 8

No forcing situation exists if the opening bidder has sharply limited his hand by a rebid of one notrump:

South	West	North	East
1 ♦	Pass	1 ♠	Pass
1 NT	Pass	2 ♥	

South is permitted to pass. He has indicated a minimum opening bid and has thus clearly warned North that a jump bid will be required to create a forcing situation.

As we have seen, the responder can force in a new suit if the opening bidder merely rebids his own suit. The force is even stronger when *both* partners bid new suits—that is, when all four suits are shown:

South	West	North	East
1 ♣	Pass	1 ♦	Pass
1 ♥	Pass	1 ♠	

Conceivably, the partnership may stop at one notrump. No great strength has been shown by either partner. However, South cannot pass one spade—the bid of the fourth suit.

Slightly more strength is shown by this bidding:

South	West	North	East
1 ♣	Pass	1 ♥	Pass
1 ♠	Pass	2 ♦	

The bid of the fourth suit is forcing, and the partnership is now at the level of two. If North had a mediocre hand he would have bid one notrump, two hearts, or two clubs rather than a new suit.

Still greater strength is shown when the responder reverses or makes his second bid at the level of three:

South	West	North	East
1 ♠	Pass	2 ♣	Pass
2 ♦	Pass	2 ♥	

Most tournament experts play a reverse by the responder as forcing to game. North has not merely the 10 points required for a minimum response at the two-level; he has enough for a second strength-showing bid. North should have at least 13 points in high cards (perhaps slightly less if his distribution is exceptionally good); and since South has an opening bid, the partnership must keep bidding until game is reached.

The message is essentially the same when the responder makes his second bid at the level of three:

South	West	North	East
1 ♠	Pass	2 ♦	Pass
2 ♥	Pass	3 ♣	

In many cases North shows the fourth suit with the intention of raising one of his partner's suits later on. The responder thus bids two suits of his own and raises his partner's suit, showing extreme shortness in the fourth suit. This is a way that the experts have of making a mild slam try without going beyond the level of game.

Assume that the bidding has begun thus:

South	West	North	East
1 ♠	Pass	2 ♦	Pass
2 ♥			

You are North, with the following hand:

♠ 2   ♥ Q J 5 4   ♦ K Q 7 6 3   ♣ A 8 4

A raise to four hearts doesn't quite do justice to this hand. If you go past game, however, you may be in jeopardy. The solution is to bid three clubs at this point and raise the hearts at your next turn. Your partner should read you for the ace of clubs, a good diamond suit, and fine support for hearts, and he can decide for himself whether the partnership has any chance for a slam.

DECEPTIVE BIDDING

Many players make deceptive bids at rubber bridge, but the gentle art of swindling is not as highly developed there as it is in duplicate. When a swindle backfires, as must occasionally happen, the loss at rubber bridge may be of major importance; at duplicate, however, it is just one board. Moreover, a deceptive bid at rubber bridge may net you only an unimportant overtrick; at duplicate, however, every trick is important.

The inexperienced player thinks of a deceptive bid as a psychic bid made with a very weak hand. Few experts make such bids with any degree of regularity; and many of them practically *never* psych. The commonest type of deceptive bid is made with a *good* hand.

For example, suppose your partner opens the bidding with one spade. You hold:

♠ 5 3   ♥ K Q 9   ♦ 8 6 3   ♣ A K J 7 5

The orthodox bid is two clubs. At your next turn, presumably, you will bid two notrump. If you get to game at notrump, a diamond opening lead may give you trouble.

The deceptive method is to bid two *diamonds* instead of two clubs. Whether or not your partner raises diamonds, you expect to bid notrump next. It's very unlikely that your partner is going to take you to four or five diamonds instead of three notrump. If you can discourage the diamond opening lead, you may not only gain time but may also thoroughly confuse the defense.

This style of bidding is not without its risks. You occasionally land in three notrump and miss a cold slam in your strong minor suit. Or your partner has an unusual hand and does get you past three notrump in the phoney minor. Or a skeptical opponent leads the phoney minor in spite of your bid, thus wrecking a hopeless notrump contract that other pairs were clever enough to avoid.

Risky or not, it's worth an occasional try. Moreover, you must reckon with the possibility that your opponents may be doing it to *you* whenever the auction goes in that fashion.

The opening bidder may try the same sort of monkey business:

South	West	North	East
1 ♦	Pass	1 ♠	Pass
?			

South has:

♠ J 5   ♥ K Q 9   ♦ A Q J 7 5   ♣ Q 6 2

One notrump is a slight underbid, two notrump is a very bad overbid, two diamonds is orthodox. The crafty bid is two clubs. This bid has the advantage of hinting at extra strength and may also discourage a club lead against the eventual notrump contract that you have in mind.

If your partner passes two clubs, you will probably have a bad score on that one board. This sort of bid should, however, earn you far more points than it loses.

The phoney suit may be bid after partner has raised your major suit. This is done to confuse the defense when your object is to get to game in the major *whatever* your partner does.

South	West	North	East
1 ♠	Pass	2 ♠	Pass
?			

You, South, hold:

♠ A K J 7 5   ♥ K J 2   ♦ A Q 6   ♣ 9 3

The orthodox bid is four spades. The crafty bid is three clubs, with the intention of getting to four spades willy-nilly. If you get a heart or diamond opening lead, well and good. If the opponents believe that you have some sort of biddable club suit, the defensive errors may persist throughout the play.

You wouldn't make such a bid with a hand that isn't worth

an eventual game contract. For example, in the same bidding situation, you might hold:

♠ K Q 9 7 5   ♥ K J 2   ♦ A Q 6   ♣ 9 3

You're not sure whether or not to bid four spades. You need your partner's help in deciding, and you must therefore tell him the truth. A bid of three spades is probably best, but you couldn't be criticized if you bid three hearts or three diamonds instead. You *would* be criticized if you bid three clubs, since that would probably steer your *partner* in the wrong direction.

If you make it a practice to open only five-card majors, you must inevitably bid three-card minor suits very often. Such bids make it difficult for the opponents to bid if they happen to have the minor suit that you have already bid. It isn't your chief purpose to talk the opponents out of their best suit, but it often has that delightful effect.

It isn't always necessary to accomplish this by accident. You may "steal" the enemy's suit by design. For example:

South	West	North	East
1 ♥	Pass	?	

You, North, hold:

♠ 5   ♥ K J 7 6 3   ♦ 9 8 4 2   ♣ K Q 8

What should you bid? Four hearts is the orthodox bid, but this may have the effect of provoking East into a stab at four spades. This is particularly dangerous if you are vulnerable against non-vulnerable opponents.

The crafty bid is one spade. You will raise hearts at your next turn, and you will eventually wind up at four hearts. The opponents must be both skeptical and courageous to try a sacrifice in spades after you have bid the suit!

You can't, however, afford to make such a bid in a suit that is higher than your real suit unless your partner will give you an inch or two of rope. For example, if South is the kind of player who will just go on taking you back to spades no matter how often you bid the hearts, you must forgo this particular deceptive bid.

It is much safer when your true suit is higher than the phoney suit:

South	West	North	East
1 ♥	Pass	?	

You, North, hold:

♠ K Q 9   ♥ K Q 7 5   ♦ 4 2   ♣ J 10 7 6

The crafty bid is two diamonds. You will raise hearts later, thus showing a two-and-a-half heart hand and also stealing the enemy's diamond suit.

Similarly, you may respond to an opening bid of one spade with a phoney response of two hearts. However, the need for evasive action isn't so great when your side has the spade suit. It's when *they* have spades that you must try to steal their suit.

One of the most ancient and moth-eaten gags in the bridge player's repertoire is the phoney bid over a takeout double:

South	West	North	East
1 ♥	Double	1 ♠	

This is a very suspicious sounding bid. If North later shows support for hearts, there is good reason to wonder whether he has any kind of spade suit at all. North might well bid one spade on such a hand as:

♠ 5 4   ♥ K Q 8 5   ♦ 7 6 3   ♣ 8 7 3 2

If he is doubled at one spade, he will run out to two hearts. If he is not doubled, he may talk the enemy out of their best suit.

This is so well known a ruse, however, that you can't expect to get away with it against experienced opponents. The following auction is far less well known:

South	West	North	East
1 ♦	1 ♥	Pass	1 ♠

East may have a real spade suit, to be sure, but he may instead have a weak hand with fair support for hearts, such as:

♠ 6 3 ♥ Q J 9 7 ♦ 7 6 3 ♣ K 7 3 2

East has only 6 points in high cards and suspects that his partner has only a mediocre hand since he merely overcalled. With a good hand, presumably, West would have doubled for a takeout or would have made a jump bid. Hence East suspects that the hand belongs to the enemy and that their best suit is spades. East gambles that *somebody* will bid or double, so that he will have a chance to get back to hearts. If he isn't vulnerable, he can even afford to play the hand at one spade undoubled and go down five or six tricks. The penalty of 250 or 300 points will be less than the value of the enemy's game in spades!

Deceptive cue-bids may be made when you are approaching a slam contract. The normal procedure is to bid a suit in which you hold the ace. The crafty course is to bid a suit in which you have only a weak doubleton or so. If the opponents fail to lead your weak suit, you may have time to develop your slam-going tricks in peace and comfort.

This kind of deceptive bidding is not as important at duplicate as at rubber bridge. If it takes a deceptive bid and a favorable opening lead to assure the slam, you can probably get a fair score without bidding the slam. It's all right to take such risks when you need some good scores towards the end of a duplicate, but it's not ordinarily sound procedure.

5. Competitive Bidding at Duplicate

THE THEORY OF DEFENSIVE BIDDING

When an opponent opens the bidding, the odds are rather high that the hand belongs to the enemy. If it doesn't, the chances are that the opponents will stop bidding at a rather low level. Your general course, in duplicate, is to wait and see what happens.

If the opponents bid confidently to a game or to a *high* part score, you keep out of the auction. When you and your partner pass throughout such an auction, one of your opponents will play the hand for nine or more tricks without the slightest clue to the location of the missing high cards. At many other tables, the declarer will be guided by the bidding of his opponents. His contract will be the same, but he will average a trick better because of the information that has been given to him.

If the opponents stop at the seven- or eight-trick level, you or your partner must pause before the final pass and decide whether or not to intervene. In many cases the last man to speak will reopen the bidding; and in some of these cases, he will find that he has stepped into a buzz-saw. Nevertheless, this course will salvage many hands and will sometimes push the opponents just one trick too high instead of allowing them to make a plus score.

This, at any rate, is the theory of defensive bidding for *balanced* hands. When your hand is *unbalanced,* however, you tend to enter the auction promptly, provided, of course, that the hand has some sort of strength in addition to the favorable distribution. Depending on the sort of strength you have, you enter the auction with a simple overcall, a jump overcall, a takeout double, or a cue-bid in the enemy's suit.

The general theory breaks down, likewise, when your hand is balanced but exceptionally strong. You can't afford to stay out of the auction with 16 points or more in high cards (except, perhaps, when you are non-vulnerable against vulnerable opponents) because your partner will have too little strength to act in the event that he is the last player to speak.

REOPENING THE BIDDING

Let's examine a few typical bidding sequences:

South	West	North	East
1 ♥	Pass	Pass	?

East should take action of some sort unless he is especially well provided with hearts. We'll come later to the *kind* of action that East should take.

South	West	North	East
1 ♥	Pass	1 NT	Pass
2 ♥	Pass	Pass	?

East should incline towards reopening the bidding. The hand may well belong to his side.

South	West	North	East
1 ♥	Pass	1 ♠	Pass
2 ♠	Pass	Pass	?

East should incline towards reopening the bidding.

South	West	North	East
1 ♥	Pass	1 NT	Pass
3 ♥	Pass	Pass	?

East should tend to stay out. The opponents have already climbed to the level of three on a hand that probably belongs to them. That's high enough.

North	East	South	West
1 ♥	Pass	1 ♠	Pass
2 ♦	Pass	2 ♥	Pass
Pass	?		

East should tend to stay out. When the opponents have bid three suits, it is often difficult to find a safe spot. Unless East has a fairly strong holding in the unbid suit, he should leave well enough alone.

There are many other similar situations, but this will convey the general idea. The last man to speak tends to reopen when the opening side has stopped at the level of two. He is allowed to pass, and does so if he is loaded in the enemy's trump suit; or if the opponents have bid too many suits; or if his own hand is hopelessly weak.

We have stated that East should tend to reopen the bidding in most of these situations without giving much thought to the strength of the East hand. The reason is that we're not greatly concerned with the strength of the *East* hand; we're concerned much more with the strength of the *East-West* cards.

When North-South stop at a low level, they probably have very little more than 20 points in high cards. If North-South had close to 26 points, they would be bidding game or at least getting to the level of three. If North-South have only 20 points or so, the remaining 20 points of the deck must be in the East-West hands.

It doesn't much matter how those 20 or so points are divided between East and West, provided that both partners are aware of the situation. The last man to speak doesn't rely on his own hand for the purpose of reopening the bidding; he relies on the strength of the *combined* hands. He is bidding his partner's hand as well as his own.

The purpose of reopening the bidding is to make a part score if possible; or to lose only 50 or 100 points for being set one trick; or to push the opponents to the level of three. The reopener's partner should not lose sight of these aims. If the opponents take the push, the job has been done. In most cases it is the wildest folly to bid again or to double the opponents. Even though the reopener's partner (West, in all the cases we have diagrammed) may have a rather good hand, he must remember that his hand has already been bid!

The last man to speak can usually indicate his strength by choosing between a bid and a double as his way of acting. A double should show about 10 points in high cards as a minimum; a bid should show less than 10 points in high cards. When the hand gets down to about 5 points, the last man usually passes instead of acting.

Assume that the bidding has been:

South	West	North	East
1 ♥	Pass	Pass	?

What should East do with each of the following hands?

♠ K Q 6 3   ♥ 4 2   ♦ A Q 4   ♣ 7 5 3 2
Double. The reopening double shows 10 or more points.

♠ K 8 6 3   ♥ 4 2   ♦ A 9 4   ♣ 7 5 3 2
Bid one spade. The hand is too weak for a double, but you mustn't sell out to a bid of only one heart.

♠ 4 2   ♥ Q J 9 5 3   ♦ A 9   ♣ 7 5 3 2
Pass. It's too bad that the opponents haven't gotten any higher, but perhaps you will do well enough against even *one* heart. It's far too dangerous to look for a way of pushing them.

♠ 4 2   ♥ Q J 9 5 3   ♦ A 9   ♣ K 5 3 2

Pass if the opponents are vulnerable; double if they are not vulnerable. You hope to collect 200 points against vulnerable opponents. If the opponents are not vulnerable, however, you cannot be satisfied with a mere 100 points; and you double in order to work towards a part score of your own.

Now let's look at it from a different point of view:

South	West	North	East
1 ♥	Pass	Pass	1 ♠ or Double
Pass	?		

What should West do with each of the following hands if East reopens with one spade, or if East reopens with a double?

♠ A J 6 5 4   ♥ 8 7   ♦ K 7 2   ♣ A 6 4

Pass if your partner bids one spade; but bid one spade if your partner doubles. If your partner bids one spade he must have a maximum of 9 points; and you have only 11 points. Game is out of the question, so you pass one spade. If necessary, you will take a push up to two spades. If your partner doubles, he shows 10 points or more. Game is remote unless your partner can raise to *two* spades.

♠ A J 9   ♥ Q 10 8 7   ♦ K 7 2   ♣ A 6 4

Pass if your partner bids one spade, or bid one notrump. You have 14 points in high cards, but your partner has 9 at most, and the chance for game is very remote. If your partner reopens with a double, pass for penalties unless you are vulnerable against non-vulnerable opponents—in which case you bid two notrump.

Let's take a reopening situation in which there has been more of an auction:

South	West	North	East
1 ♥	Pass	2 ♥	Pass
Pass	?		

What should West do with each of the following hands?

♠ K J 8 6   ♥ 5 3 2   ♦ Q J 7   ♣ 6 4 3

Bid two spades. Perhaps you can push the enemy one trick higher. You may even be able to make two spades if allowed to play there. In this situation some experts will boldly bid a *three-card* spade suit on the theory that neither opponent is likely to have enough spades for a double!

♠ K J 8 6   ♥ 5 3 2   ♦ Q J 7   ♣ A 4 3

Double. The reopening double shows 10 points or more. This may get you in trouble, of course, but you can't afford to play too cozy in this situation.

And now from the other position:

South	West	North	East
1 ♥	Pass	2 ♥	Pass
Pass	2 ♠	3 ♥	?

What do you, East, do with each of the following hands?

♠ Q 10 9 7 5   ♥ 4   ♦ K 8 4   ♣ K J 5 2

Pass. You have 9 points in high cards and your partner has a maximum of 9. With a combined count of 18 points you are not anxious to bid for nine tricks in spite of the good distribution.

♠ Q 10 9 7 5   ♥ 4   ♦ K 8 4   ♣ A Q J 2

Bid three spades. This hand may well belong to your side. If the opponents go on to four hearts, you will be willing to double. Despite the strength of this hand you cannot afford to go to game. Your partner has counted on much of this strength when he bid two spades.

♠ Q 7 5 3 2   ♥ - - -   ♦ K 10 8 4   ♣ A K J 2

Bid four spades. It's very unusual to take your partner's reopening bid to a game, but it isn't impossible. You need a very strong hand, an excellent fit, and tremendous distribution. Don't do it with less!

♠ 10 9 7   ♥ Q J 9 4   ♦ K 8 4   ♣ A 5 2

Pass. Don't even dream of doubling three hearts for penalties! You should be delighted that the opponents are up so high and that your partner has been enterprising enough to push them. You will probably defeat three hearts, but you cannot be sure of this. You should have a good score even if you don't double, provided that you beat them. If you double them and fail to beat them, however, you will not only have a bottom but you will also convince your partner that he can't afford to reopen the bidding in this sort of situation.

SIMPLE OVERCALLS

The simple overcall shows a good trump suit of five or more cards and unbalanced distribution. If the trump suit isn't good, you may have a takeout double or a pass, but you don't have an overcall. If the distribution is balanced, you probably have a sound pass rather than an overcall. As we have seen, in duplicate bridge you can afford to wait with most balanced hands until the opponents have stopped bidding.

Let's try some examples:

South	West	North	East
1 ♥	?		

What do you, West, do with each of the following hands?

♠ K Q J 7 3   ♥ 8 5 2   ♦ 6 4 2   ♣ 7 6

Pass. There's no great harm in a bid of one spade, but there's also no great virtue in it. If you avoid bidding with wretched hands of this nature, your partner will be able to assume that you really have something when you do overcall.

♠ K Q J 7 3   ♥ 2   ♦ 9 6 4 2   ♣ K 7 6

Bid one spade. The hand has been strengthened both in distribution and in high cards. It is now worth some action.

♠ K J 7 3 2   ♥ 2   ♦ K 6 4 2   ♣ K 7 6

Pass. Don't overcall with a bad trump suit. Part of the

reason for overcalling with a *good* trump suit is that you want to take the strain off your partner just in case he is the last man to speak and has only two or three small cards in your good suit. You are announcing that your trump suit is satisfactory opposite such meagre support. In this case, you cannot afford to make that announcement.

♠ K Q J 7 3   ♥ 5 2   ♦ A 4 2   ♣ K 7 6

Bid one spade. The distribution is balanced, but the suit is good and the strength is rather high. You'd like to stay out, but this may put too much strain on your partner if he is last to speak.

♠ K Q J 7   ♥ 8 5 2   ♦ A 4 2   ♣ K 7 6

Pass. There is no excuse for coming in with a four-card suit and balanced distribution. You would need about 16 points in high cards to act immediately with this distribution.

RESPONDING TO A SIMPLE OVERCALL

If your partner is a sound overcaller, you can respond to his overcalls very much as though he had opened the bidding with a suit that was known to be long and strong. The overcall will usually represent a hand of 12 to 14 points, counting distribution as well as high cards.

You can well afford to raise a major suit with three small trumps, provided that your hand as a whole is strong enough. There is little point in bidding a new suit when you have support for your partner's overcall; your bid will not be considered forcing, and you may find yourself in the wrong contract. (Some experts require somewhat stronger hands for an overcall, and treat almost any takeout as forcing for one round. This method is quite playable, but the last player may be expected to reopen the bidding with very slight values. This method is fine for experts but is difficult for the average player to handle.)

In counting your hand for support of your partner, beware of counting strength in the enemy's suit, unless you are *behind* the bid. You can afford to pass any hand of less than 10 points (unless you want to make a deceptive bid, as we'll see). With about 10 or 11 points you can afford to make some sort of bid. With about 12 or 13 points you can afford to make a highly invitational bid. With more than 13 points, you must insist on a game.

Let's apply these principles:

South	West	North	East
1 ♥	1 ♠	Pass	?

What do you, East, do with each of the following hands?

♠ 8 6　　♥ 7 3 2　　♦ K J 9 4　　♣ A Q 5 3

Pass. You have 10 points in high cards, to be sure, but you have no reason to think that any contract is better than one spade. You can't raise spades, can't bid notrump, and have no suit of your own to bid. Pass such hands quickly in the hope that the enemy will overbid.

♠ 8 6 5　　♥ 7 3　　♦ K Q 9 4　　♣ A Q 5 3

Bid two spades. You can afford to think about a raise since you have three trumps. You count 11 points in high cards but cannot really afford to count much for the doubleton with only three trumps in your hand.

♠ 8 6 5　　♥ 7　　♦ K Q 9 4 2　　♣ A Q 5 3

Bid three spades. You have 11 points in high cards and can afford to count about 2 points for distribution. (You would count 3 points if the three of clubs were made the three of spades.) You can practically demand a game, but you give your partner a bit of leeway just in case he has stretched hard to make his overcall. Don't bid the diamonds, for your partner may have to pass; and then you will be in a miserable minor instead of a magnificent major.

♠ J 8 6 5   ♥ 7   ♦ K Q 9 4 2   ♣ A Q 5

Bid four spades. This hand ought to produce a good play for game opposite any reasonable overcall.

♠ 8 6   ♥ K J 7   ♦ K Q 9 4   ♣ Q 10 5 3

Bid one notrump. You have 11 points in high cards and your partner should have an equal amount. You have balanced distribution and a stopper in the enemy's suit. Notrump ought to be a fine contract, and the level seems to be right for the combined strength.

♠ 8 6   ♥ K J 7   ♦ K Q 9 4   ♣ A J 5 3

Bid two notrump. You have 14 points in high cards, and your partner should have about 11 or more. If he has full value in high cards he will raise notrump, and you will have a good play for your game. If he has a minimum overcall, he can afford to pass.

♠ 8 6   ♥ 7 3   ♦ A Q J 9 4   ♣ K 9 5 3

Pass. Your partner is probably as well off in spades as you would be in diamonds. Avoid going from a major to a minor when there is any choice in the matter.

♠ 6   ♥ 7 3   ♦ A Q J 9 8 4   ♣ K 9 5 3

Bid two diamonds. You have a good suit of your own and lack support for your partner's suit. This sort of takeout is a *denial*.

♠ J 8 6 5   ♥ 7   ♦ Q 9 4 2   ♣ 9 6 5 3

Bid something. Your partner probably has only 11 or 12 points in high cards, and you have only 3 points. Obviously, the opponents have about 26 of the 40 points in the deck, and you must try to talk them out of their game. A raise to two spades is the mildest sort of action to take. If you have the courage of your convictions you might try a jump raise to *three* spades.

JUMP OVERCALLS

In rubber bridge the jump overcall is best used to show a good hand and a good suit. It can be used for this purpose in duplicate also, but most match-point experts prefer to use the jump overcall as a sort of shutout bid. When they have the *good* hand, they double for a takeout and then bid the strong suit at the next opportunity.

The pre-emptive jump overcall is used to show a long suit in a hand that is comparatively without defensive strength. The total strength of the hand varies with the vulnerability.

South	West	North	East
1 ♥	?		

What do you, West, do with each of the following hands?

♠ K J 10 8 6 5 ♥ 5 2 ♦ J 10 8 3 ♣ 4

Bid two spades if not vulnerable. The hand will probably produce about five tricks and the opponents will not get rich doubling it, particularly if they are vulnerable. If you are vulnerable, pass. (Players who make light overcalls may bid *one* spade with this hand.)

♠ K J 10 8 6 5 ♥ 5 2 ♦ K J 8 3 ♣ 4

Bid two spades if both sides are vulnerable. You will probably take six tricks with this hand. If you are not vulnerable, you may bid either one or two spades.

♠ K Q 10 9 6 5 2 ♥ 5 ♦ K J 8 3 ♣ 4

Bid one spade. There will be more bidding, and you'll have the chance to show more strength. If your partner is properly respectful of vulnerability, you may jump to two spades with this hand if vulnerable against non-vulnerable opponents. There is practically no such bid with a weak hand, so the strength is adequately shown to an understanding partner.

♠ 6 5　　♥ 5　　♦ K J 10 8 6 5 2　　♣ Q 4 3

Bid three diamonds if not vulnerable. If vulnerable, however, pass.

♠ Q 4 3　　♥ 5　　♦ K J 10 8 6 5 2　　♣ 6 5

Pass in any vulnerability. Don't make a shutout bid in diamonds when you have good support for a major suit.

♠ 6 5　　♥ 5　　♦ A K J 8 6 5 2　　♣ Q 4 3

Bid three diamonds vulnerable. There isn't much use for such a bid except to show a very powerful suit that will produce about seven tricks with just a little help. This bid, used in this way, invites your partner to try for game in notrump if he can help solidify your suit and can stop the enemy's suit and at least one other suit. In short, he needs a few top cards and a little help in diamonds.

THE TAKEOUT DOUBLE

The takeout double is used by duplicate experts mostly on unbalanced hands and exceptionally strong balanced hands. The moderately strong balanced hand is better managed with a simple pass.

Players who use jump overcalls for shutout use a takeout double as the first step in showing a strong suit in a strong hand.

South	West	North	East
1 ♥	?		

What do you, West, do with each of the following hands?

♠ K J 7 4　　♥ 2　　♦ K Q 9 3　　♣ A J 6 5

Double. This is a "book" double, with unbalanced distribution, excellent support for all unbid suits, and 14 points in high cards. If all takeout doubles were like this bridge players would have fewer gray hairs.

♠ K J 7 4   ♥ 2   ♦ K Q 9 3   ♣ Q J 6 5

Double. This is a shaded double, since you have only 12 points in high cards. You make the best of your 12 points since in every other respect—distribution and support for all unbid suits—the hand is ideal for a takeout double.

♠ Q J 7 4   ♥ 2   ♦ K Q 9 3   ♣ Q J 6 5

Pass. You have to draw the line somewhere, and this is a good place to draw it. Don't make a takeout double with only 11 points in high cards, no matter how ideal the hand is in other respects. Moreover, beware of making a strength-showing bid when you have no ace and only one king. (The 4-3-2-1 count is usually accurate, but it slightly overstates the value of queens and jacks; so you have to be wary of hands that are very short of aces and kings.)

♠ K J 7 4   ♥ 5 2   ♦ K Q 9   ♣ A J 6 5

Pass or double. You tend to pass if your partner has the courage of a mountain lion when it comes to reopening the bidding. You tend to double if your partner is timid about reopening. If your partner is neither bold nor timid (or if you're not sure about his nature), you have a borderline decision.

♠ K J 7   ♥ 5 2   ♦ K Q 9 3   ♣ A J 6 5

Pass. The decision is no longer borderline when you have doubtful support for the unbid major. There is practically no such thing as *never* in bridge, but this comes pretty close to it: Never make a takeout double without either strong support for the unbid major or a *very* good suit of your own.

♠ 5 2   ♥ K J 7   ♦ K Q 9 3   ♣ A J 6 5

Pass. See the previous hand.

♠ K 2   ♥ K J 7   ♦ K Q 9 3   ♣ A J 6 5

Bid one notrump. The hand is now too strong for a pass, but it is still unsuited to a takeout double. An overcall of one notrump (showing about the same sort of hand as a standard opening bid of one notrump) best describes it.

♠ A K J 7 4 3   ♥ 2·   ♦ K Q J 9   ♣ A 6

Double. You will show the spades at your next turn, thus indicating a strong suit in a strong hand.

♠ K Q J 7 4 3   ♥ 2   ♦ K Q J 9   ♣ A 6

Double. Here again you will bid the spades at your next turn. This a near-minimum holding for this method of bidding.

♠ K Q J 7 4 3   ♥ 2   ♦ Q J 9 3   ♣ A 6

Bid one spade. The hand is not strong enough for a takeout double first and then a spade bid.

♠ K Q J 7 4 3   ♥ – – –   ♦ K Q J 9   ♣ A K 6

Bid two hearts. This immediate cue-bid in the enemy's suit demands a takeout and is forcing to game. The hand is too strong for a takeout double!

♠ A K J 7 4 3   ♥ 2   ♦ K Q J 9   ♣ A K

Bid two hearts. When the hand is otherwise strong enough you can afford to make this kind of cue-bid even though you have a loser in the enemy's suit.

♠ A K J 7 4 3   ♥ 3 2   ♦ K Q J   ♣ A K

Double. You intend to bid the spades at your next turn. Practically no hand is strong enough for a cue-bid in the enemy's suit when you have a worthless doubleton in that suit.

RESPONDING TO A TAKEOUT DOUBLE

You respond to a takeout double in duplicate much as you do in rubber bridge. You try a little harder, perhaps, for the unbid major or for a notrump contract. You avoid stretching for a free response, since this show of strength may lure your partner into a penalty double.

South	West	North	East
1 ♥	Double	Pass	?

What do you, East, do with each of the following hands?

♠ 9 7 2 ♥ J 8 6 3 ♦ 7 5 4 ♣ 9 7 2

Bid one spade. When your only four-card suit is the enemy's, bid the cheapest three-card suit. Some experts would bid two clubs with this sort of hand, preferring not to "lie" about the unbid major. Whatever you do, bid. You have a fair chance of escaping disaster if you bid; practically none at all if you pass for penalties with a worthless hand.

♠ 7 2 ♥ J 8 6 3 ♦ 7 5 4 ♣ 9 7 3 2

Bid two clubs. Don't try to get out of trouble with the "cheapest" bid in a doubleton suit. If you're worried about this hand, take comfort from the fact that many other players will hold it. You don't need a miraculous result; you need only to do as well as all the other unfortunate souls who share your problem.

♠ 9 7 3 2 ♥ 6 4 ♦ J 8 6 3 ♣ 7 5 4

Bid one spade. You cannot be delighted with this hand, but you don't worry when you can make a normal response in the unbid major.

♠ 9 7 3 2 ♥ 6 4 ♦ Q J 8 6 3 ♣ 5 4

Bid one spade. It's dollars to doughnuts that your partner has four-card support for spades. Don't wander into a mediocre minor suit when the major will probably produce just as good a part score.

♠ 9 7 3 2 ♥ 6 4 ♦ K Q J 6 3 ♣ 5 4

Bid two diamonds. It's reasonable enough to bid a strong five-card minor rather than a weak four-card major. If your partner bids spades next, you will raise. If your partner passes, there is a fair chance that you will have the chance to try two spades at your own next turn. If everybody passes two diamonds (unlikely in a good game), this is probably as good a contract as any.

♠ Q J 3 2   ♥ 6 4   ♦ A Q J 6   ♣ 7 5 4

Bid two spades. The jump response invites your partner to bid towards game. He will accept the invitation if he has a respectable takeout double. He will pass discreetly if he has stretched badly for his double.

♠ K Q 10 8 3   ♥ 6 4 3   ♦ A 6   ♣ 7 5 4

Bid two spades. As in the previous case, the jump response is highly invitational. You often have a good five-card suit, as in this case; but you sometimes have a four-card suit, as in the previous case.

♠ Q J 3 2   ♥ 6 4   ♦ A Q J 6   ♣ K 5 4

Bid two hearts. This cue-bid in the enemy's suit is forcing to game. Such a cue-bid is more often used, when the opponents have bid a minor suit, to indicate a willingness to play at game in either major suit.

♠ 6 4   ♥ Q J 5   ♦ K 8 6 3   ♣ Q 7 6 2

Bid one notrump. This response shows a stopper in the enemy's suit with about 6 to 10 points. Good players never make this bid with a really bad hand.

♠ 6 4   ♥ K J 5 2   ♦ K 8 6   ♣ K Q 6 2

Bid two notrump. This response shows a probable double stopper in the enemy's suit, balanced distribution, and about 11 to 13 points in high cards. (With 14 or more you would cue-bid the enemy's suit or jump to *three* notrump.) Your partner should accept the invitation to game even if he has stretched to make his double.

♠ 6 4   ♥ Q J 10 9 7   ♦ K 8 6   ♣ 7 5 4

Pass. The penalty pass shows length and strength in the enemy's suit, with three probable trump tricks. Outside strength is desirable but not essential. You want your partner to lead a trump, and you want to lead trumps at every opportunity. In effect, you want to play this hand as though you were declarer—drawing trumps to safeguard your partner's high cards in the side suits.

♠ 6 4   ♥ Q 9 8 6 3   ♦ K 8 6   ♣ 7 5 4

Bid two clubs. The hearts are not strong enough for a penalty pass, and the hand as a whole is not strong enough for a response of one notrump. Hence you try to scramble to safety in the cheapest three-card suit.

BIDDING OVER THE TAKEOUT DOUBLE

When your partner's opening bid is doubled for a takeout, you redouble with 10 points or more. Any bid other than a redouble shows less than 10 points.

If your hand is not good enough for a redouble, you may make an *improving* bid in a good suit. Thus you may bid a fairly good five-card major suit, particularly if there is some danger that you won't get another inexpensive chance to bid the suit. You may, instead, bid one notrump to show about 7 to 9 points with balanced distribution.

With support for your partners' suit, you may raise as a sort of shutout bid. A double raise is not a strong bid in this situation; *only a redouble shows strength.*

The redouble ranges from 10 points to 20-odd points (in the case of a psychic takeout double). The redoubler may be ready to double the enemy, to support the opening bid, or to bid a new suit. He will rebid at a minimum level with close to 10 points, but will rebid with a jump of some kind with 13 points or more.

South	West	North	East
1 ♥	Double	?	

What do you, North, do with each of the following hands?

♠ 7 6 3   ♥ 9 4 2   ♦ 8 5 3   ♣ J 8 7 6

Pass. The best way to indicate weakness is to pass.

♠ 7 6 3   ♥ J 9 4 2   ♦ 8 3   ♣ K 8 7 6

Pass. You are not a bit worried about a heart contract, but the hand is too weak for any action.

♠ 7 6 3   ♥ Q J 4 2   ♦ 8 3   ♣ K 8 7 6

Bid two hearts. This raise shows heart support and a total of about 6 or 7 points, including distribution.

♠ 7 6 3   ♥ Q J 4 2   ♦ 3   ♣ K J 8 7 6

Bid three hearts. The double raise in this situation shows trump support and a count of 8 to 10 points, including distribution.

♠ 7 3   ♥ Q J 5 4 2   ♦ 3   ♣ K J 8 7 6

Bid four hearts. The triple raise in this situation shows fine trump support with more than 10 points all told, but with insufficient high-card strength for a redouble.

♠ K Q 9 8 4   ♥ 5 2   ♦ 8 3   ♣ Q J 8 6

Bid one spade. If you wait, your next chance to bid may require you to bid two or three spades, and your hand won't be strong enough for that. You must therefore bid the spades now or never.

♠ K Q J 8 4 2   ♥ 5 2   ♦ 8   ♣ Q J 8 6

Pass. The hand is not strong enough for a redouble, but you can afford to bid the spades later at a high level. It will then be clear to your partner that you could afford to wait, and he will get a proper impression of your strength.

♠ 7 6 3   ♥ 2   ♦ 8 5 3   ♣ K Q 10 9 8 6

Bid two clubs. The takeout at the level of two suggests extreme shortness in the major suit (singleton at most) and a strong six-card suit of your own.

♠ 7 6 3   ♥ 2   ♦ 8 5 3   ♣ Q J 8 6 5 3

Pass. Don't "rescue" in a weak suit. The odds are very high that the opponents will bid; or that your partner will be as well off at one heart as you would be at two clubs.

♠ Q 6 3   ♥ 5 2   ♦ K 8 5 3   ♣ K 8 7 6

Bid one notrump. If you pass, you may never get a convenient chance to show your strength, such as it is. The bidding may be up to two spades or two of a minor when your next turn comes and you will then have no convenient bid. As a result, the enemy may steal the hand. This would be no great misfortune in rubber bridge, where a pass might be your best action; but you can't afford to let the enemy steal a hand in duplicate.

♠ K J 6 3   ♥ 5 2   ♦ K J 8   ♣ A 8 7 6

Redouble. You intend to double any further bid by the opponents. If you are vulnerable against non-vulnerable opponents, you may bid two notrump at your next turn instead of doubling. It would be pleasant to have a somewhat better hand, but you would redouble even with a point or two less.

♠ 6 3   ♥ K J 4 2   ♦ 8 3   ♣ A K 8 7 6

Redouble. You intend to raise to three hearts at your next turn. The chances are that you will merely get to game, but the redouble shows your true strength and reveals the situation if the takeout double is psychic. For all you know, there may be a slam in the hand.

♠ 6 3   ♥ 5 2   ♦ K Q 8 3   ♣ A K J 7 6

Redouble. You expect to bid clubs at your next turn, unless you get the chance to double a minor-suit contract. In the meantime your redouble shows that you have 10 points or more. Conceivably, your partner may double a spade contract before your next turn comes, relying on your redouble for high-card strength and on his own spades for trump tricks. You will be willing to accept the double if not vulnerable against vulnerable opponents; but otherwise, you will probably try for game in notrump.

COOPERATIVE PENALTY DOUBLES

The penalty double brings in bushels of points at rubber bridge, and bushels of match points at duplicate. In both games you must use the penalty double of a low contract as a suggestion. If your partner can co-operate in the defense against this low contract, he passes your double; otherwise he finds a rebid of some kind.

The situation arises most typically when your partner opens the bidding and the next player overcalls. You double with any good balanced hand that seems to have no very clear future. You do *not* double with length in the enemy's suit but no other strength of any kind.

You may naturally ask: What is a good balanced hand? How good does it have to be?

The answer depends on your trump strength. You count on your partner to furnish three defensive tricks, so you need enough additional tricks in your own hand to defeat the contract. The more trump tricks you have, the less you need elsewhere.

Another factor to be considered is vulnerability. If you are vulnerable against non-vulnerable opponents, you are not likely to collect enough to compensate you for a game. You avoid doubling in this vulnerability unless a very good part of your strength is in the enemy's trump suit. (Even then you should at least consider a game at notrump.)

A third factor is the extent to which you fit your partner's suit. If you have a singleton in his suit, the partnership values will be well adapted for defense. If you have three or four cards in your partner's suit, your defense is weakened and your offensive strength is increased.

A fourth factor is the height of the contract. You may be reluctant to double a contract of one, willing to double a contract of two, and eager to double a contract of three.

These various factors are illustrated in the examples that follow.

South	West	North	East
1 ♥	2 ♣	?	

What do you, North, do with each of the following hands?

♠ K 6 2   ♥ 5 2   ♦ A Q 7 3   ♣ Q 10 8 4

Double. You will probably win two club tricks and two or three side tricks. If your partner wins his three promised tricks, you will set two clubs. You will almost surely collect more than the value of a part score, and your side may well have no game.

♠ K J 2   ♥ 5 2   ♦ A K J 3   ♣ 10 8 7 4

Double. If you do not win a trump trick, your trumps have great nuisance value. You should be able to win four tricks in the side suits in any case.

♠ 5 2   ♥ K J 2   ♦ A K J 3   ♣ 10 8 7 4

Bid two diamonds. You avoid a penalty double with a weak trump holding when you have a fine fit for your partner's suit. You intend to raise hearts at your next turn.

♠ Q 6 2   ♥ 5 2   ♦ 8 7 3   ♣ K J 10 7 4

Pass. It is useless to double clubs when you are not in the least prepared for any other contract. Why warn the enemy of the only danger that you can cope with? What's more, a double of two clubs is very unlikely to stand; you and the bidder should have ten or eleven clubs between you, and *somebody* is bound to be short in clubs. His partner—or yours—will probably take the double out.

When a low penalty double of this kind is made, the doubler's partner should tend to pass with fair defensive values but should bid again if very short in the doubled suit or if most of his strength is concentrated in a 6-card or longer suit.

South	West	North	East
1 ♥	2 ♣	Double	Pass
?			

What do you, South, do with each of the following hands?

♠ A 7 5   ♥ A K J 8 4   ♦ Q 10 9   ♣ 5 2

Pass. You have balanced distribution and should easily take the three defensive tricks that your partner is counting on.

♠ A 7 5   ♥ A K J 8 4   ♦ Q 10 9 2   ♣ 5

Bid two diamonds. Do not pass a cooperative double with a singleton trump. As an exception, you might pass with a singleton king or ace provided that the rest of the hand was good for defense.

♠ A 7   ♥ A K Q 8 4 3   ♦ 9 5 2   ♣ 5 2

Bid two hearts. So much of your strength is in the six-card suit that you may not win the three defensive tricks that your partner is counting on. Therefore you rebid the strong suit.

♠ A Q 5   ♥ A K Q J 4 3   ♦ 9 5 2   ♣ 5

Bid three hearts. You can't afford to pass because of the unbalanced distribution and the concentration of strength in hearts. The jump rebid is necessary to show that you have substantially more than a minimum opening bid. If your partner has doubled largely on side strength, you may well have a slam in this hand; and the jump bid will alert your partner to that possibility.

COMPETITIVE PENALTY DOUBLES

When both sides get up to the level of three or higher, it is possible that both sides are safe but it is more likely that one side is overbidding. If the hand belongs to your side, you must double the opponents when they get overboard.

It is impossible to describe in complete detail how to know when the opponents are overboard. No matter how good your judgment is in this respect you are bound to be wrong some of the time.

You must base your decision partly on a conviction that the hand belongs to your side, for it is usually a needless risk to double the opponents when the hand is theirs. (You will probably get a good score even without doubling whenever the opponents *overbid* a hand that belongs to them.) In addition to believing that the hand is yours, you must also be reasonably sure that you have bid as far as you can safely go. Finally, you must have strength in the enemy's suit or general defensive strength.

By the time you have reached this stage you should have a pretty accurate idea of the combined strength in points on hands that get you up to the level of three or higher. If you have only 20 points or so, the hand doesn't clearly belong to either side. If you have a combined count of 22 or more points, the opponents will have only 18 points or less; and then the hand belongs to your side.

If *all* of your competitive doubles turn out well, you are not doubling often enough! Experts don't play safe in this situation.

LEAD DIRECTING DOUBLES

In several situations it is necessary to double a bid or a final contract to indicate a lead to your partner. You double specifically for this purpose rather than for the general purpose of increasing the penalty. (When the hand belongs to the enemy, as we have several times observed, you will get a good result for any plus score regardless of whether or not you have doubled.)

A double of three notrump calls for the following lead:

(a) The doubler's suit if he has bid a suit.

(b) The leader's suit if he has bid and if the doubler hasn't bid.

(c) The first suit bid by the dummy if the defenders haven't bid.

If you expect to beat three notrump by means of some *other* lead, don't double.

A double of a voluntary slam contract calls for an *unusual* lead. If the doubler has bid a suit, he does *not* want that suit led. If the leader has made the only defensive bid, the double asks him to lead a different suit. A slam double never calls for a trump lead.

The doubler will often have a void suit and be anxious to get a ruff on the opening lead. The opening leader should consider this possibility carefully and pick a likely suit. If no such possibility seems to exist, the leader should lead the first side suit bid by the dummy.

If you expect to defeat a slam contract by means of a *normal* lead, don't double.

You are sometimes able to indicate a favorable lead by doubling some early bid rather than the final contract. Thus, you may double a cue-bid or a conventional bid of some kind. When you make such a double you must be ready not only for the opening lead but also for a surprise decision of the opponents to redouble and stay there. Hence you need length as well as strength in the suit that you double.

South	West	North	East
1 ♠	Pass	3 ♠	Pass
4 ♣	Pass	4 ♦	Double

East has reason to believe that a diamond lead will work well against the eventual final contract. East should have something like K-Q-J-x-x in diamonds.

South	West	North	East
1 NT	Pass	2 ♣	Double

North's bid is part of the Stayman Convention. North usually does not have a club suit, but is merely asking the no-trumper to show a major suit if he has one. East's double shows length and strength in clubs; and it asks West to lead a club if he is the eventual opening leader.

South	West	North	East
1 NT	Pass	2 ♣	Pass
2 ♦	Double		

South's bid is part of the Stayman Convention, announcing that he does not have a biddable major suit. South may or may not have a biddable diamond suit. West's double shows length and strength in diamonds; and it asks East to lead a diamond if he is the eventual opening leader.

6. Special Bidding Conventions

Most duplicate players use one or more special bidding conventions to help them reach the best contracts. In League tournaments, all contestants are required to keep these conventions prominently displayed on the table. In most club games, there is little explanation of the conventions used by the players.

Even though you may play in a duplicate club where few players bother to explain their conventions, you should become familiar with all of the special gadgets in common use. You may decide to adopt some of them, or you may merely wish to understand what the opponents are doing when they seem to be making peculiar bids.

THE BLACKWOOD CONVENTION

The Blackwood Convention is a method of showing aces and kings wholesale instead of one at a time. The idea is to bid makable slams and stay out of unmakable slams.

When either member of the partnership bids four notrump as a conventional bid (we'll soon come to the question of when the bid is conventional) he asks his partner to reply according to the following schedule:

With no ace or with all four aces............five clubs
With one ace ....five diamonds
With two aces ....five hearts
With three aces ....five spades

In most cases the player who has bid four notrump will know immediately how high he wants to bid. If he decides to bid only five of some previously bid suit, he is assumed to know what he is doing. He must know that the opponents hold two aces and that a small slam is therefore impossible.

Sometimes the first response reveals that only one ace is missing. The *captain* (the player who has bid four notrump) then goes right to six in the suit that he fancies best. On rare occasions, the captain discovers that all of the aces are accounted for and that a grand slam is a possibility. He may then find out about his partner's kings by bidding five notrump, which asks for a reply according to the following schedule:

With no king or all four kings..................six clubs
With one king ....six diamonds
With two kings ....six hearts
With three kings ....six spades

A player who has been asked only about his aces should not question the captain's choice of final contract. The captain knows how many aces are missing; the partner does *not* know.

A player who has been asked about kings, however, does know that all of the aces are accounted for. (The captain should not bid five notrump unless the partnership holds all four aces.) The partner may occasionally go on to seven if the captain stops short. This is correct if the partner holds considerable trump strength and a very strong side suit. The partner knows that a king is missing since the captain has failed to bid a grand slam, but the partner has reason to believe that the missing king will have nothing to do with the grand slam.

Most experts use four notrump as a conventional Blackwood bid only if notrump has not previously been bid by the partnership. Some experts prefer to agree that *any* bid of four notrump is Blackwood. Still other experts allow some bids to be conventional but rule out others. All of these methods have their advantages and their disadvantages.

When you are playing with your favorite partner, make sure that both of you clearly understand which bids of four no-trump are conventional. When you are playing with an unfamiliar partner the safest course is to treat any bid of four notrump as conventional.

When you are disappointed in your partner's response to four notrump and decide not to go to slam, you may wish to play the hand at a final contract of five notrump. If you bid five notrump directly, your partner will tell you all about his kings—which interests you not at all.

The solution is to bid a *new* suit at the level of five, if possible. (If no new suit is available, or if the new suit cannot be bid at the level of five—give up! You will have to play the hand in a suit.) Such a bid, useless for ordinary purposes, asks your partner to bid five notrump—which you intend to pass.

For example:

West	East
♠ Q 8 3	♠ K J 5
♥ A Q 10 4 3	♥ K J
♦ A J 8 7	♦ K Q 10 9 6
♣ 4	♣ K Q 9

West	East
1 ♥	3 ♦
4 ♦	4 NT
5 ♥	5 ♠ !
5 NT	Pass

East naturally tries for a slam, particularly when his partner shows diamond support. When West can show only two aces, however, East must abandon the slam. East can bid a new suit, spades, at the level of five to scramble into five notrump. West fortunately knows the convention and obliges. Five notrump, easily makable, should be the top normal spot.

THE GERBER CONVENTION

The Gerber Convention closely resembles the Blackwood in aims and methods. It begins with a bid of four clubs instead of four notrump. Partner responds according to the following schedule:

With no ace or all four aces..................four diamonds
With one ace ....four hearts
With two aces ....four spades
With three aces ....four notrump

In the best version of this convention, the *captain* asks for kings by bidding *five clubs*. Kings are shown in the same way, except that they are one level higher.

Many experts use the Gerber Convention when the partnership has previously bid notrump. Some experts use Gerber "when obvious," meaning when a jump is made to four clubs at a time when it would be nonsensical except as part of the Gerber Convention.

THE FISHBEIN CONVENTION

The Fishbein Convention is a method of doubling for penalties when an opponent opens with three of a suit. The double of an opening three bid by the next player is a *business double*. Some other bid must be found, of course, for the equivalent of a takeout double. That way is by means of the "cheapest suit" bid.

Suppose, for example that South opens the bidding with three diamonds. West can double for penalties if he hopes that will be the final contract. West can bid three hearts to demand a takeout, not necessarily showing a heart suit. West can bid three spades or four clubs as natural bids. West can bid three notrump, hoping to play it there. (Note that an overcall of three notrump is a natural bid; the cheapest *suit* is used to demand a takeout.)

If West has bid three hearts, asking for a takeout, East should respond as though to a takeout double. East should make a *jump* response to game if he has moderate strength. For example, East would jump to four spades with:

♠ K J 7 6 4　　♥ K 5 3　　♦ 8 6 2　　♣ Q 3

The Fishbein Convention applies only to the player who speaks immediately after the shutout bid. The ordinary co-operative double is used by the player who speaks last:

South	West	North	East
3 ♦	Pass	Pass	?

If East doubles, he is asking for a takeout; but West may convert it into a penalty double by passing. East is not likely to have a good penalty double since his trumps are under those of the bidder. Hence the double is used for takeout.

Any bid by East has its natural meaning. If he bids three hearts, he has a good heart suit and a hand strong enough for this bid. And so on.

WEAK TWO BIDS

Some experts use the opening bid of two in a suit as a sort of pre-emptive bid instead of as a forcing bid. A few of these players use weak two bids in all suits; but most reserve the opening bid of two clubs as a forcing bid.

The typical weak opening two bid is a hand that contains a fairly strong six-card suit but that is not quite strong enough for an ordinary opening bid. For example:

♠ 6 3　　♥ A Q J 8 7 4　　♦ K 8 5　　♣ 7 3

Bid two hearts, if using weak two bids.

The responder may raise the opening bid, may bid a new suit, may bid some number of notrump, or may pass. Any takeout is forcing for one round, but a raise is not forcing. Some experts use a simple raise as an invitation to game, and others use it as a bid that must be passed.

A favorite stunt of a crafty responder is to bid a weak suit in the hope of confusing the enemy. The next player may be able to expose such a bid by doubling.

There is no general agreement on the exact nature of the opening two bid. Many experts decline to make such a bid with strength in an unbid major, with strength in three suits, or with less than a good six-card suit. Other experts refuse to restrict themselves in any such way.

The general defense against an opening two bid is the co-operative double, much as if the opening bid were *three*. Some players use the Fishbein method over weak two bids. Others use three clubs as a demand for a takeout, using all other calls in their natural meaning.

TWO CLUBS AS A FORCE TO GAME

Many experts use two clubs as the only or as the principal forcing opening bid. Such an opening bid shows:

(a) an ordinary forcing two-bid in some suit, not necessarily clubs; *or*

(b) a very strong notrump hand of more than 22 points.

The responder doesn't know, at first, which type of hand the opener has. The opener will clarify the situation at his second turn.

The responder uses two diamonds as a weakness response. He may bid two hearts, two spades, three clubs or *three* diamonds to show a minimum of about 7 points and some sort of biddable suit. He may bid two notrump to show a balanced hand with about 7 points or slightly more. (With 10 points or more, the responder should bid a suit first.)

After the responder has bid, it is up to the opening bidder to clarify his story. If he bids a suit, he announces that he has the ordinary kind of two-bid in that suit. If he bids notrump, he announces that he has the very strong notrumper.

South	West	North	East
2 ♣	Pass	2 ♦	Pass
2 ♠			

South has the sort of hand that would call for a two-spade bid in most systems. He already knows that his partner has a weak hand (less than 7 points). North may now show some sort of long suit without unduly encouraging his partner. For example, North would first bid two diamonds and then three hearts with:

♠ 8 5   ♥ K J 9 6 5 3   ♦ 6 3 2   ♣ 5 3

After South has bid his true suit the bidding continues in the familiar way. North shows a suit if he has one, or raises the opener's suit with trump support, or bids notrump—until at least game is reached. This does not differ materially from the way the bidding develops after an ordinary forcing bid of two.

The big difference comes when the opener has a big notrump hand. At his second turn, the opening bidder may bid a minimum number of notrump or he may make a jump bid in notrump. Each shows a different point count.

Instead of bidding a strong notrump hand in this way, the opener may open with two notrump or with three notrump. This gives him four different bids, and each can be used to show a different number of points. In each case, the opener needs balanced distribution and all four suits stopped.

Type of bid	Points
Opening of 2 NT	21 or 22 points
Opening 2 ♣; minimum rebid in NT	23 or 24 points
Opening 3 NT	25 or 26
Opening 2 ♣; jump rebid in NT	27 or 28

In each case the opening bidder's hand is shown within one point. The responder can easily see whether or not there is a chance for slam by adding his own points to the number shown by the opening bidder.

A further advantage of the method is that the opening bid of two notrump is broken down into two stages. If the opener bids two notrump to begin with, the responder can afford to pass with a very bare 3 or 4 points. If the opener bids two clubs first and then two notrump, however, the responder should go on to game with the bare 3 or 4 points. With only 2 points (or less), the responder may now pass.

JACOBY TWO BIDS

Oswald Jacoby has devised a very good method of distinguishing between two different types of two-bid.

An opening bid of two spades, two hearts, or two diamonds indicates a very good suit in a hand that is good enough to force to game. Moreover, there is a singleton or a void somewhere in the hand.

An opening bid of two clubs, however, shows:

(a) a big notrump hand, as just explained; *or*

(b) a very good club suit in a game-forcing hand, with a singleton or void somewhere; *or*

(c) any very good suit (not necessarily clubs), with no singleton or void anywhere in the hand.

The responder bids normally in response to two spades, hearts, or diamonds. As the bidding develops, however, the responder must beware of attaching great importance to his own long suit (if he has one) unless raised. The chances are that this is the opener's singleton or void.

Contrariwise, the responder can afford to give some weight to his own long suit if the opening bid has been two clubs. The opener guarantees two or more cards in each suit.

ACES OVER TWO BIDS

My personal opinion is that the convention known as aces-over-two-bids is the worst ever devised by the mind of man. It must be admitted, however, that some very fine players swear by this method.

The central idea is very simple. If your partner opens with a two-bid, you bid any suit in which you have an ace. If you have no ace, you must bid two notrump willy nilly.

There are all sorts of different ideas about what to do if you have more than one ace; or what to do at your second turn after you have shown one ace or no ace at your first turn. Some players show their kings next; others show a biddable suit, if possible.

Fortunately this situation is rare, so you won't often be puzzled when your opponents bid aces over two bids. If you use it yourself and find yourself puzzled, don't say I didn't warn you!

SHEINWOLD TWO BIDS

If you *must* show aces over two bids, the best compromise is my own convention. The idea is to make a game-forcing bid that tells your partner whether you are more interested in his aces or in his distribution and general strength.

About nine-tenths of your two bids will consist of two-suiters, semi-two-suiters, and three-suiters. You will want your partner to help you choose the final trump suit. After he has done so, you will then try to find out about aces—if the bidding encourages you to think about a slam.

With any such hand you open with a bid of two clubs. If your second bid is in a suit, your partner knows that you have a game-forcing hand and a strong suit but that you want him to make normal responses. (If your second bid is in notrump, your partner knows that you have the big notrump sort of hand.)

About one-tenth of the time you will have one tremendous solid suit and some high cards on the side. You will want to force to game, and you will be interested only in your partner's aces and kings; for you already know the eventual trump suit.

With the one-suiter hand, you open with two in that suit.

This bid asks your partner to show his aces if any. If he has no aces he must bid two notrump. A responder who has bid two notrump (to show no aces) must bid a suit in which he has the king (if any) at his second turn.

Anybody who wants to make up detailed arrangements about showing more than one ace or more than one king is at liberty to do so. You get this kind of two-bid about once a year, and by the time it comes along you'll have forgotten your arrangements or you'll be playing with a partner who doesn't use this convention with you. If you do want a simple method, however, jump to three notrump at the first response to show two aces; or to four notrump to show three aces. If you show no aces at your first turn and you are then expected to show kings, bid the cheapest king first; and bid another king if you get a chance to do so below game.

I invented the convention in order to get along with partners who insist on bidding aces over two-bids. I recommend it for that purpose.

PRE-EMPTIVE JUMP RESPONSES

In the Roth-Stone system a jump response is used to show a bad hand rather than a good one:

South	West	North	East
1 ♦	Pass	2 ♠	

North has a long topless spade suit in an otherwise worthless hand. He can play the hand at spades, but nowhere else. If South happens to fit the spades, the partnership can go on to game (or, rarely, to slam). Otherwise South passes in a hurry, even with a very good hand.

This convention does not apply to a passed hand, whose jump bid is used to show a maximum pass:

South	West	North	East
Pass	Pass	1 ♦	Pass
2 ♠			

South has a good hand and a good spade suit.

WEAK NOTRUMP

Many experts use the opening bid of one notrump to show 12 to 14 points rather than 16 to 18 points. The responses are much the same as usual, except that the responder needs an additional 4 points to take any strong action.

The responder begins to think about game if he has a good 12 points or more. With only 11 points or less in a *reasonably balanced* hand, the responder must pass—quickly and calmly! The last player will often be lured into entering the auction unless warned away by a hesitant pass. The responder is anxious to have the enemy come in when he has 9 to 11 points, for he can usually collect a penalty greater than the value of his part score.

If the responder passes, the opener must leave any further developments to his partner. The opener's hand is fairly well indicated; but the responder may have anything from 0 to 11 points. If an opponent bids, the responder is the one to decide what action to take.

If the responder has a good 12 points or more, he may raise in notrump, make a jump bid in a suit, or bid two clubs (Stayman Convention). The opener makes the usual response to the Stayman bids, carries on to game over a jump response, passes a raise to three notrump, and usually goes to game if partner makes an invitational raise to two notrump.

Some players are afraid that the weak notrump will result in bad sets, but these are players who have never tried the bid. Even vulnerable you will seldom sustain a bad loss.

If you like to open only a sound opening bid, I highly recommend the weak notrump. It gives you some way of showing the balanced hand of 12 to 14 points. If your partner has a mediocre hand and unbalanced distribution he can bid two of a long suit (which you *must* pass) or pass one notrump.

If your opponents use the weak notrump, beware of doubling with a doubtful hand. It is safer to bid a suit than to double.

South	West	North	East
1 NT	Pass	Pass	2 ♦

East is fairly safe, since South is practically compelled to pass. (South may double if he has exceptionally good diamonds, but he cannot make any *bid,* and he cannot double with merely *fair* diamonds.) West has a chance to stand for diamonds or try a different suit, whereupon North may be unable to double. If East doubles instead of bidding a suit, it is up to West to make the first choice of suit. If his first choice is unlucky, North can intervene with a double, and the fat is now in the fire. Once North has shown strength with a double, South can join the party by doubling any bid that strikes his length.

UNUSUAL NOTRUMP OVERCALLS

A player who reopens the bidding may be reluctant to do so with a double for fear of encouraging his partner to bid the unbid major. The reopener may have excellent support for either minor, but poor support for the unbid major. To show this, he reopens with a bid in notrump. Since this situation occurs practically only at the level of two, the reopening bid is almost always *two* notrump.

South	West	North	East
1 ♥	Pass	2 ♥	Pass
Pass	2 NT		

West has some such hand as:

♠ 5 3   ♥ 7 2   ♦ A J 8 5 3   ♣ K Q 10 5

He wants East to bid his longer minor suit.

Other typical situations are:

South	West	North	East
1 ♠	Pass	1 NT	Pass
2 ♠	2 NT		

West intervenes at once to take the strain off his partner.

South	West	North	East
1 ♠	Pass	1 NT	Pass
2 ♠	Pass	Pass	2 NT

The last man speaks up with a request for his partner's longer minor suit.

UPSIDE DOWN DEFENSIVE SIGNALS

Karl Schneider, veteran Austrian bridge star, developed the idea of turning the usual defensive signals upside down, and a few American experts have adopted the idea.

Briefly, you play low and then high to encourage your partner to lead a suit—instead of the customary high-low. Contrariwise, you play high and then low to tell your partner *not* to lead a suit.

This convention applies only to situations where your partner needs to be told whether to lead a suit or to continue a suit. It has no effect on the trump echo (to show three trumps) or the distributional echo (to show two or four cards in a suit). It likewise has no effect on the suit preference signal. It is used only when you would normally use a "come-on" or a "stay away" signal; and in any such case it reverses the normal procedure.

The chief value of the convention is to allow you to encourage a continuation of a suit when you can't afford to spare a high card. Other benefits result from the fact that it is harder for the declarer to deceive your partner with a false card.

If you use this convention, you are required to announce it to the opponents, just like a bidding convention.

7. The Play of the Cards at Duplicate

As we have already observed in an earlier chapter, you cannot afford to play for safety in a duplicate game. If you find yourself in a *normal* contract, you must play for every trick that isn't nailed down. If you're in a *bad* contract, you must look for any desperate maneuver that may salvage a few match points from the wreckage. Only if you're in a *very good* contract can you afford to play for safety.

Let's take some typical examples:

North
♠ 9 8 7
♥ A 5 4
♦ K 6
♣ A Q J 10 8

South
♠ A K J 10 2
♥ J 6 3
♦ J 8 3
♣ K 9

The bidding:

South	West	North	East
1 ♠	Pass	2 ♣	Pass
2 ♠	Pass	4 ♠	Pass
Pass	Pass		

West opens the deuce of hearts, and you step right up with dummy's ace. You lead a trump from the dummy, and East plays low.

Should you finesse or not?

At rubber bridge you would play the ace and king of trumps. There is, after all, a fair chance that the queen will drop. If it fails to drop, you go after the clubs in the hope of getting rid of a heart or two before the opponent who has the queen of trumps can ruff in. This line of play gives you the best chance for your contract—and you are looking only for the best chance for ten tricks.

In a duplicate game, however, you can't afford to play for ten tricks when there are reasonable chances to win eleven or twelve. The contract is quite normal, so you must play for maximum.

You win the first trick with the ace of hearts, lead a trump to the ace, return the nine of clubs to dummy's queen, and lead the nine of spades for a finesse (assuming, of course, that the queen of spades didn't have the kindness to drop singleton on the first round of trumps). If the finesse succeeds, you will make five spades, five clubs, the ace of hearts, and perhaps even the king of diamonds. If the finesse loses, however, you will almost certainly go down at your game contract.

You would surely play the hand safe for four spades if you were sure that there was no reasonable chance to make five or six. You would even be willing to play safe for ten tricks if you thought that the rest of the field would do the same. You would then be no worse off than anybody else.

The trouble is that two or three pairs are likely to play this hand later in the session at a time when they are hungry for match points. They will go all out for as many tricks as possible. And so will one or two players early in the evening, either because of courage, high spirits, or optimism.

Since everybody knows that the hand will surely be played

optimistically at several tables, everybody must come to the conclusion that he will have company if he also plays it the same way. If the result is unfortunate, he will tie a few players and thus get at least two or three points.

One more argument before we leave this very important point. One or two declarers may get a favorable opening lead. For example, some luckless defender may pick this inopportune moment to open a trump from the West hand! Or perhaps somebody may open a club. The declarers who get such favorable leads will have the chance to play for overtricks without risking the game. Your only chance to tie with them is to play optimistically!

The importance of playing for overtricks may extend even to a slam:

North
♠ 10 2
♥ K Q 3 2
♦ A K 9 7 6 3 2
♣ — — —

South
♠ A J 5
♥ A J 10 9
♦ 4
♣ A K J 6 3

The bidding:

South	West	North	East
1 ♣	Pass	1 ♦	Pass
1 ♥	Pass	3 ♥	Pass
4 NT	Pass	5 ♦	Pass
5 NT	Pass	6 ♥	Pass
Pass	Pass		

West leads the three of spades, and East plays the king. You, South, naturally win the first trick with the ace of spades and look around for new worlds to conquer.

You are glad that you resisted the temptation to bid six notrump, but you are sorry that you didn't bid *seven* hearts. After a brief inspection of the partnership cards, you come to the conclusion that almost every North-South pair will play this hand at six hearts. After all, how can anybody stay out of a slam with all those high cards, such a good fit in hearts, and a void suit into the bargain?

If you were playing this hand at rubber bridge, you would play it as safe as possible for twelve tricks. The safest line of play is to cash the two top clubs, discarding a spade and a diamond from the dummy. Ruff a spade with dummy's deuce, cash the ace of diamonds, ruff a diamond, ruff another spade with dummy's trey of hearts, and then cross-ruff with high trumps. You make two clubs, one diamond, one spade, and eight trumps. You can stand a 5-0 trump break and a 4-1 diamond break. In fact, the hand is almost unbeatable.

At duplicate, however, you must take a slight risk of going down at six hearts in order to preserve the play for seven! The right play is to take the ace of spades, cash the ace of clubs to discard dummy's spade, take the ace of diamonds and ruff a diamond.

If both opponents follow to both rounds of diamonds you are practically home for thirteen tricks. You cash the ace and jack of hearts, overtake the ten of hearts in dummy, to draw any remaining trumps, and run the good diamonds. Only a 5-0 trump break can beat you if the diamonds are 3-2.

If one opponent shows out on the second round of diamonds, you need a 3-2 trump break. Cash the ace of trumps and overtake the jack of hearts in dummy. Ruff one more low diamond to establish the suit. Now ruff a spade in dummy, draw the last trump, and run the good diamonds.

You will make seven if *either* red suit breaks 3-2 as long as the other red suit is no worse than 4-1. The odds are about 9 to 1 in your favor.

You can hardly be said to be taking a great risk when you adopt a play that gives you 9 to 1 odds, but it would still be the wrong line of play in rubber bridge. In duplicate you are willing to take *slight* risks with a slam contract if the slam seems very easy to bid.

When the slam seems difficult to bid, however, you may play it safe even though you are playing duplicate:

North
♠ 10 9 7 2
♥ K Q
♦ A Q J 10 9 4
♣ 9

South
♠ A Q J 8
♥ A 8 3
♦ K 5
♣ K J 6 2

You stagger into a contract of six spades somehow or other. The exact bidding isn't important since it is bound to be optimistic at best. The combined hands have only 30 points in high cards, but the fit is very fine.

West opens the jack of hearts, and East plays the deuce of hearts at the first trick. How should you plan the play?

If you try a trump finesse, you will make either seven or five. For if West wins with the king of spades he will lead a club at once.

You should not take this risk. If you make the small slam you will have a very fine score, since the chances are that very few pairs will be bold enough to bid the slam. Hence you decide to play it safe for twelve tricks.

After winning the first trick with the queen of hearts, cash the king of hearts. Lead a trump to your ace (resisting the temptation to finesse!) and cash the ace of hearts in order to discard dummy's singleton club.

Only now can you relax and lead a second trump. If all has gone well up to this point, you have nothing to worry about.

Perhaps you may argue that it isn't *absolutely* safe to run three rounds of hearts before drawing trumps. That's true, but *absolutes* are hard to find at the bridge table. The odds are about 4 to 1 that you will be able to cash three hearts safely; and the odds are only even on the trump finesse. It is surely safer to play for a 4 to 1 shot than for an even money shot.

Now let's turn our attention to a *bad* contract.

North
♠ A J
♥ K J 10 7 5
♦ 8 7 5 3 2
♣ 8

South
♠ K 9 5
♥ A Q 8
♦ A 9 6 4
♣ K 9 6

The bidding:

South	West	North	East
1 NT	Pass	3 ♥	Pass
3 NT	Pass	Pass	Pass

West leads the deuce of clubs, and East wins the first trick with the ace. East returns the four of clubs.

Your first step is to prepare a few choice remarks to make to your partner at the end of the hand. He should be playing the hand at four hearts instead of letting you play it at three notrump! He would lose a club and one or two diamonds, making either ten or eleven tricks.

At notrump, you can run nine tricks without the slightest difficulty—five hearts, a club, a diamond, and two spades. This will probably get you only a near-bottom. You get no match points for three notrump when everybody else is making four or five hearts.

The only hope is to play for ten tricks at notrump in the hope that only ten tricks can be made at hearts. (There is no play for *eleven* tricks at notrump, so you must resign yourself to a bad score if it is possible to make eleven tricks at hearts.)

You win the second trick with the king of clubs and immediately finesse dummy's jack of spades! If the finesse loses, the defenders will run their clubs and defeat the game contract. Even if this happens, you have still made the *right* play. The score for being set will be only a point or so worse than the score for making nine tricks at notrump.

If the spade finesse works, you will have ten tricks at notrump: three spades, five hearts, a diamond, and a club. This gives you a chance for a good score. If the diamonds are obliging enough to break 3-1, the other declarers will lose two diamonds and a club, just making their ten-trick heart contracts. You will have a fine score for ten tricks at notrump, and you will compliment your partner on his risky but brilliant pass!

If you follow my advice on reopening the bidding, you will sometimes land in a dangerous contract. Don't play such hands with cold feet!

North
♠ A K
♥ 10 9 5
♦ K J 9 8 5
♣ 9 8 4

South
♠ J 9 8 5 2
♥ 4 3
♦ A Q 7
♣ 7 6 2

Neither side vul.

The bidding:

West	North	East	South
1 ♥	Pass	1 NT	Pass
2 ♥	Pass	Pass	2 ♠
Double	Pass	Pass	Pass

West leads the king of hearts and continues the suit until you ruff the third round. You lead to dummy's top trumps and note that each opponent follows to two rounds. You then get back to your hand with the queen of diamonds and wonder whether or not to lead another trump.

If you lead another trump and discover that West has both the queen and ten, you will win no more tricks! You will be down a matter of 700 points. (If West has both of the missing trumps, he will take them both, thus exhausting your trumps. He should then be able to run the rest of the tricks with hearts and clubs.)

If you lead another trump and discover that each opponent has one trump left, you can be set only one trick. The enemy will take, at most, one trump, two hearts, and three clubs. The loss will be only 100 points.

If you abandon trumps and just lead diamonds, however, the opponents will make their trumps separately, whether they are split or together. You will be set two tricks, for a loss of 300 points.

There's no doubt about the correct procedure at rubber bridge—assuming that you were foolish enough to make this kind of bid in rubber bridge! You should settle for 300 points. It doesn't pay to risk 400 points more in the attempt to save only 200 points.

You would decide it the other way in duplicate, however. You simply can't afford to go down 300 points. That will be just about as bad a bottom as being minus 700 points. Your only chance is to play the hand wide open in the hope of restricting the loss to 100 points. Hence you lead the third trump like a little man.

Incidentally, you may even make this contract! If the trumps break, West may lead another heart instead of switching to clubs. He may think that his partner has the ace of diamonds —which is why you play the *queen* rather than the ace of diamonds in returning to your hand. If West does make the mistake of leading another heart, you will ruff and run the diamonds, making your doubled contract with an overtrick!

The rubber bridge player prides himself on his knowledge of safety plays. The duplicate player may know them, but he seldom uses them. For example, take the following typical situation:

North
♠ A Q 8
♥ A 5
♦ A 10 6
♣ K 9 4

South
♠ K 7 3
♥ K 4
♦ K Q 7
♣ A J 5 3 2

The bidding:

South	West	North	East
1 NT	Pass	6 NT	Pass
Pass	Pass		

West opens the queen of hearts. You can confidently expect to win three spades, two hearts, and three diamonds. Hence you need four club tricks to make sure of the contract.

If you were playing the hand at rubber bridge, your course would be clear. You would win the first trick in either hand, cash the ace of clubs, and lead a low club towards dummy.

If West followed to the second round of clubs with queen

or ten, you would have no problem. If West showed out on the second round of clubs, you would go up with the king and lead the dummy's last club back through East's queen-ten.

If West followed to the second round of clubs with a *low* club, you would finesse dummy's nine! This is the standard safety play with the combination of A-J-x-x-x opposite K-9-x.

You don't mind losing that trick to East, whether he happens to win with the queen or with the ten. If East can win the trick, the clubs must be 3-2, and dummy's king will clear the suit on the next round.

If East *cannot* win the trick, your safety play has paid off. West must have started the hand with Q-10-x-x of clubs, and only the safety play has saved you from defeat.

All of these thoughts go through your mind when you play this hand at duplicate, but you still don't try to execute the safety play. You must play a low club to dummy's king and finesse the jack on the next round in the attempt to make all thirteen tricks.

The whole field will be playing it that way, and you can't afford to be the only prudent pigeon who managed to lose a club trick with the queen onside.

Does this mean that the safety play has no place in duplicate bridge? Not quite. You make safety plays when you are doubled and can thus assure the contract; or when your contract is highly satisfactory for other reasons. You don't make safety plays at normal contracts—even slams.

DEFENSIVE PLAY

Defensive play at duplicate follows slightly different lines. If the contract is normal, you play for whatever tricks can be won without great risk. If the contract is abnormally good for *your* side, you nurse your tricks carefully to make sure that you get enough for a good score. If the contract is abnormally good for the enemy, there isn't much you can do—but you are willing to try almost anything!

North
♠ 7 3 2
♥ 10 6 2
♦ K J
♣ K J 9 3 2

West
♠ A
♥ A K J 7
♦ A 8 3 2
♣ 8 7 6 4

The bidding:

South	West	North	East
1 ♠	Double	Pass	2 ♥
3 ♠	4 ♥	4 ♠	Pass
Pass	Pass		

You, West, lead the king of hearts and continue at the second trick with the ace of hearts. South ruffs with a low trump and leads the king of spades to your ace.

What should you lead next?

It is evident that you are going to make only one spade and one heart. You need two tricks in the minor suits to defeat the contract. All will be well if your partner has a club trick, but if declarer's clubs are solid you need two diamond tricks to defeat four spades.

At rubber bridge you would lead a small diamond in the hope that your partner has the queen and that declarer will finesse the jack instead of putting up the king. If declarer happens to guess right, your partner will still lead a diamond if he gets in with a high club. And if your partner cannot get in with a high club, you are never going to beat this contract except by giving South a chance to guess wrong on a diamond lead.

At duplicate, you cannot afford to play all out to defeat the contract. It is obvious that South has the ace of clubs for his opening bid and that you may never get the ace of diamonds if you fail to lay it down immediately. You must "cash out" instead of trying to defeat the contract.

The situation would be different if you were defending against four spades *doubled*. You cannot then afford to settle for three defensive tricks, for the double will guarantee a fine score to North-South. You must lead a low diamond through dummy's king-jack and hope for the best.

The principle is illustrated also in the following hand, taken from the 1954 Master Pair Championship:

```
                        North
                      ♠ Q 9
                      ♥ A 10 7 6 2
                      ♦ A Q J 6
                      ♣ 10 6
      West                              East
    ♠ A J 10 6 3                      ♠ 4 2
    ♥ 5 3                             ♥ J 8 4
    ♦ 8                               ♦ 10 9 7 5 4 3
    ♣ J 9 8 4 3                       ♣ Q 7
                        South
                      ♠ K 8 7 5
                      ♥ K Q 9
                      ♦ K 2
                      ♣ A K 5 2
```

The bidding:

North	East	South	West
1 ♥	Pass	1 ♠	Pass
2 ♦	Pass	4 NT	Pass
5 ♥	Pass	6 NT	Pass
Pass	Pass		

West opened the four of clubs, East put up the queen, and

South won with the king. South next led the five of spades towards dummy.

At rubber bridge, West should play low and await developments. West doesn't expect to set the contract, but he sees no point in making matters easy for South.

In a duplicate game, West cannot afford to duck. If he doesn't take his ace of spades he may never get it!

As a matter of fact, several West players ducked at the second trick and lived to regret it. Declarer won in dummy with the queen of spades and ran the hearts and diamonds, discarding three spades and a club from his own hand. At the end, West had to bare down to *two* cards and couldn't save the ace of spades together with the jack-nine of clubs! Whatever he discarded, declarer had the last two tricks.

The play to prevent overtricks sometimes begins with the opening lead. At rubber bridge you often lead low from K-J-x-x-x against a notrump contract because your best chance to set the contract is to strike a supporting honor in your partner's hand. At duplicate you usually avoid such leads for fear of giving declarer a free finesse and an overtrick.

The leads and plays that are available to you as a defender are the same as in rubber bridge, but the *objective* is not necessarily the same. In most cases you must play to prevent overtricks rather than to defeat the contract; and this change of aim may have a profound effect on what you lead or play when you have any kind of choice.

8. Conducting a Small Duplicate

A large tournament is a highly technical matter that should be left to professionals, but it's easy to organize and conduct a small duplicate in your home. You need a set of duplicate boards, some scoring equipment, a little general knowledge, and an appropriate number of bridge players.

TWO TEAMS

The simplest—and the most instructive—contest for you to organize is a total point contest for two teams. You need only eight players (more can be used, if some are willing to take turns in sitting out), two tables—preferably in different rooms, pencils, ashtrays, and at least four sheets of lined paper.

The first job is to select the two teams. Appoint two captains, let them toss a coin to determine who has first pick, and then let them each select a player in turn. If you don't want to embarrass the players who are selected last, have the captains go into another room to make their selections.

Put half of one team North-South at one table and the other half East-West at the other table. Be sure to check this while the first board is being played at each table. It's pure waste of time to let the same team sit North-South at each table, but you'd be surprised to learn how often this elementary mistake is made.

Decide in advance how many boards you will have time to play. Experienced players will usually take five or six minutes per board in this kind of contest, so that a session of 28 boards should take about three hours, allowing for intermission and delays of various kinds. A session of 32 boards is just a trifle too long for beginners, but fine for experienced players.

Assuming that you have decided on a contest of 28 boards, put boards 1-7 on Table I and boards 8-14 on Table II. Let the players shuffle and deal all the boards in advance, since this is faster than doing it as the boards come up.

The two tables should finish play at about the same time. You can then exchange the boards, so that each table plays the boards that were previously played at the other table. If one table finishes far ahead of the other, you can pass over the finished boards and let the quicker table get started.

When the first fourteen boards have been played at both tables, let the two teams compare scores. The scores may be kept on the printed forms made up for this purpose or on any sheet of lined paper. Just rule off a few columns, leaving room for the number of the board, the contract, and the result (plus or minus).

A team will usually be plus at one table and minus at the other table. If the plus exceeds the minus, it has won the difference; otherwise it has lost the difference. If it is plus at both tables, it wins the sum of both scores. If it is minus at both tables, it loses the sum of the two scores.

The two teams will want to compare scores and argue a bit at the halfway mark, after the play of the first 14 boards. This is the time to put in reserves if an extra player has been sitting out. This is also a good time to think of refreshments.

After an appropriate interval, not more than fifteen or twenty minutes, start the second half. Let one team keep its original seats, and have the other two pairs change tables. Distribute boards 15-21 to Table I and boards 22-28 to Table II.

Check once more to make sure that each team is sitting North-South at one table and East-West at the other.

At the end of the second half, let the two teams compare scores again. Remember to add in the results of the first half. The team with a plus score for the entire 28 boards is the winner.

THREE TEAMS

The preliminaries and general method are the same as the contest for two teams. However, you need three tables, each with four chairs and other equipment, such as ashtrays. Moreover, it's handy to have a set of boards numbered from 1 to 42 or more.

Assuming that you want to play only 28 boards in all, and that you have only the standard 32-board-set, put boards 1-7 on Table I, boards 8-14 on Table II, and boards 15-21 on Table III. Instruct team No. 1 to sit together temporarily at Table I; team No. 2 at Table II, etc. Then have the East-West pair of each team move to the next higher-numbered table: from I to II, from II to III, and from III to I.

The players are now ready to shuffle the boards and begin to play. Make sure that all arrows point to the side of the room that you have announced as North.

Don't move any boards or let any players wander around until all three tables have finished. Then have the East-West pairs move once more to the higher table. Move the boards in the opposite direction: from I to III, from III to II, and from II to I.

At the end of the second move, you will find that each team has played two matches of 7 boards each. Give them an intermission to discuss and argue, and then have each team sit once more at its original table. By way of variety, you might let the original North-South players sit East-West for the second half, and vice versa.

Put the same boards out for the second half, and let the teams copy exactly the moves of the first half. Be sure to turn one card face up in each board before distributing them in order to make sure that all boards are shuffled.

At the end of the second half, compare scores once again. If each team wins one of its matches, there is no sure way to say who is the final winner, but you've all had a lot of fun.

FOUR PAIRS

Number your pairs from 1 to 4. Label your two tables I and II. Indicate which wall of the room is North. Use boards 1 to 27, and use printed traveling scoreslips. There are three rounds in the contest.

First round: Pair 4 is N-S at Table I, against Pair 1. At Table II, Pair 2 is N-S against Pair 3. But boards 1-3 on Table I, boards 4-6 on Table II, and boards 7-9 on an end table between the two tables. The table that finishes first exchanges boards with the end table, after which the other table can make a similar exchange. Both tables play all nine boards. At the end of the first round, all the scoreslips can be match-pointed: the higher N-S score gets 1 point, and the lower 0; the higher E-W score likewise gets 1 point, and the lower 0; if the scores are a tie, each pair gets ½ point.

Second round: Pair 4 is at Table I N-S against Pair 2. At Table II, Pair 3 is N-S against Pair 1. Distribute boards 10-18 in the same way as in the first half. Score in the same manner.

Third round: Pair 4 is still at Table I N-S, against Pair 3. At Table II, Pair 1 is N-S against Pair 2. Distribute boards 19-27 in the usual way and score in the usual way.

Add each pair's total of match points. The highest total determines the winner.

SIX PAIRS

You need three tables, 12 players, and printed scoreslips. There are five rounds, since each pair will play one round against each of the other five pairs. In the simplest arrangement, 6 boards are played during each round. All of the boards are played at each of the tables during the same round, and they therefore go out of play immediately and can be scored then and there. A 30-board game is a bit on the long side, so the director (or host) should caution the players from time to time against long discussions and other delaying tactics.

Arrange the tables, if possible, in a row and announce that North is in the direction of that row. Let the players take any seats, provided that partners sit opposite each other in the usual way. Then tell them their pair numbers according to the following diagram:

NORTH

Pair 6 (N-S)

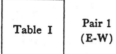

Table I   Pair 1 (E-W)

Pair 5 (N-S)

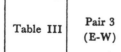

Table II   Pair 2 (E-W)

Pair 4 (N-S)

Table III   Pair 3 (E-W)

Whichever pair sits E-W at Table I is called Pair 1. Consult the diagram to see which number belongs to each pair.

Pair 6 remains N-S at Table I during all five rounds of the contest. The other pairs move to a different place for each round. That place is always the seats that were occupied during the previous round by the next-lower-numbered pair.

Before the play of the first round begins, ask Pair 2 to look at Mr. and Mrs. so-and-so (give the actual names of the players that are Pair 1) and to notice where they are sitting. During the second round, Pair 2 will sit where Pair 1 sat for the first round; and they must then look around to see where Pair 1 is sitting in order to know where they sit on the next round. This continues for all five rounds. Pair 2 *follows* Pair 1.

When you have explained this principle aloud, announce also which pair is *followed* by all of the other pairs. Pair 3 will follow Pair 2 (have Pair 2 stand up for a second or two so that Pair 3 can remember who they are). Continue this kind of identification: Pair 4 follows Pair 3; Pair 5 follows Pair 4; Pair 6 stays put; and Pair 1 follows Pair 5.

Players who listen to your announcement will be able to find the right places for all five rounds. Just in case you have a scatter-brain or two in your little group, use this schedule to solve your problems if some pair comes to you late in the game and asks which seats to play at:

	Table I		Table II		Table III	
	N-S	E-W	N-S	E-W	N-S	E-W
Round 1	6	1	5	2	4	3
Round 2	6	2	1	3	5	4
Round 3	6	3	2	4	1	5
Round 4	6	4	3	5	2	1
Round 5	6	5	4	1	3	2

During the first round, put boards 1-2 on Table I, 3-4 on Table II, and 5-6 on Table III. Tell the players to shuffle the boards and to begin play. When Table III has finished its boards, it passes them to Table II; and when Table II has finished its boards, it passes them to Table I; and Table I passes to Table III. In this way, each table can play all six of the boards in an orderly progression. When all have been played at all three tables, the round is over, and the change may be called.

INDEX

A CATALOG OF SELECTED
DOVER BOOKS
IN ALL FIELDS OF INTEREST

A CATALOG OF SELECTED
DOVER BOOKS
IN ALL FIELDS OF INTEREST

DRAWINGS OF REMBRANDT, edited by Seymour Slive. Updated Lippmann, Hofstede de Groot edition, with definitive scholarly apparatus. All portraits, biblical sketches, landscapes, nudes. Oriental figures, classical studies, together with selection of work by followers. 550 illustrations. Total of 630pp. 9⅛ × 12¼.
21485-0, 21486-9 Pa., Two-vol. set $29.90

GHOST AND HORROR STORIES OF AMBROSE BIERCE, Ambrose Bierce. 24 tales vividly imagined, strangely prophetic, and decades ahead of their time in technical skill: "The Damned Thing," "An Inhabitant of Carcosa," "The Eyes of the Panther," "Moxon's Master," and 20 more. 199pp. 5⅜ × 8½.   20767-6 Pa. $4.95

ETHICAL WRITINGS OF MAIMONIDES, Maimonides. Most significant ethical works of great medieval sage, newly translated for utmost precision, readability. Laws Concerning Character Traits, Eight Chapters, more. 192pp. 5⅜ × 8½.
24522-5 Pa. $4.50

THE EXPLORATION OF THE COLORADO RIVER AND ITS CANYONS, J. W. Powell. Full text of Powell's 1,000-mile expedition down the fabled Colorado in 1869. Superb account of terrain, geology, vegetation, Indians, famine, mutiny, treacherous rapids, mighty canyons, during exploration of last unknown part of continental U.S. 400pp. 5⅜ × 8½.   20094-9 Pa. $7.95

HISTORY OF PHILOSOPHY, Julián Marías. Clearest one-volume history on the market. Every major philosopher and dozens of others, to Existentialism and later. 505pp. 5⅜ × 8½.   21739-6 Pa. $9.95

ALL ABOUT LIGHTNING, Martin A. Uman. Highly readable nontechnical survey of nature and causes of lightning, thunderstorms, ball lightning, St. Elmo's Fire, much more. Illustrated. 192pp. 5⅜ × 8½.   25237-X Pa. $5.95

SAILING ALONE AROUND THE WORLD, Captain Joshua Slocum. First man to sail around the world, alone, in small boat. One of great feats of seamanship told in delightful manner. 67 illustrations. 294pp. 5⅜ × 8½.   20326-3 Pa. $4.95

LETTERS AND NOTES ON THE MANNERS, CUSTOMS AND CONDITIONS OF THE NORTH AMERICAN INDIANS, George Catlin. Classic account of life among Plains Indians: ceremonies, hunt, warfare, etc. 312 plates. 572pp. of text. 6⅛ × 9¼.   22118-0, 22119-9, Pa., Two-vol. set $17.90

ALASKA: The Harriman Expedition, 1899, John Burroughs, John Muir, et al. Informative, engrossing accounts of two-month, 9,000-mile expedition. Native peoples, wildlife, forests, geography, salmon industry, glaciers, more. Profusely illustrated. 240 black-and-white line drawings. 124 black-and-white photographs. 3 maps. Index. 576pp. 5⅜ × 8½.   25109-8 Pa. $11.95

THE BOOK OF BEASTS: Being a Translation from a Latin Bestiary of the Twelfth Century, T. H. White. Wonderful catalog of real and fanciful beasts: manticore, griffin, phoenix, amphivius, jaculus, many more. White's witty erudite commentary on scientific, historical aspects enhances fascinating glimpse of medieval mind. Illustrated. 296pp. 5⅜ × 8¼. (Available in U.S. only) 24609-4 Pa. $6.95

FRANK LLOYD WRIGHT: Architecture and Nature with 160 Illustrations, Donald Hoffmann. Profusely illustrated study of influence of nature—especially prairie—on Wright's designs for Fallingwater, Robie House, Guggenheim Museum, other masterpieces. 96pp. 9¼ × 10¾. 25098-9 Pa. $8.95

FRANK LLOYD WRIGHT'S FALLINGWATER, Donald Hoffmann. Wright's famous waterfall house: planning and construction of organic idea. History of site, owners, Wright's personal involvement. Photographs of various stages of building. Preface by Edgar Kaufmann, Jr. 100 illustrations. 112pp. 9¼ × 10. 23671-4 Pa. $8.95

YEARS WITH FRANK LLOYD WRIGHT: Apprentice to Genius, Edgar Tafel. Insightful memoir by a former apprentice presents a revealing portrait of Wright the man, the inspired teacher, the greatest American architect. 372 black-and-white illustrations. Preface. Index. vi + 228pp. 8¼ × 11. 24801-1 Pa. $10.95

THE STORY OF KING ARTHUR AND HIS KNIGHTS, Howard Pyle. Enchanting version of King Arthur fable has delighted generations with imaginative narratives of exciting adventures and unforgettable illustrations by the author. 41 illustrations. xviii + 313pp. 6⅛ × 9¼. 21445-1 Pa. $6.95

THE GODS OF THE EGYPTIANS, E. A. Wallis Budge. Thorough coverage of numerous gods of ancient Egypt by foremost Egyptologist. Information on evolution of cults, rites and gods; the cult of Osiris; the Book of the Dead and its rites; the sacred animals and birds; Heaven and Hell; and more. 956pp. 6⅛ × 9¼. 22055-9, 22056-7 Pa., Two-vol. set $21.90

A THEOLOGICO-POLITICAL TREATISE, Benedict Spinoza. Also contains unfinished *Political Treatise*. Great classic on religious liberty, theory of government on common consent. R. Elwes translation. Total of 421pp. 5⅜ × 8½. 20249-6 Pa. $7.95

INCIDENTS OF TRAVEL IN CENTRAL AMERICA, CHIAPAS, AND YUCATAN, John L. Stephens. Almost single-handed discovery of Maya culture; exploration of ruined cities, monuments, temples; customs of Indians. 115 drawings. 892pp. 5⅜ × 8½. 22404-X, 22405-8 Pa., Two-vol. set $17.90

LOS CAPRICHOS, Francisco Goya. 80 plates of wild, grotesque monsters and caricatures. Prado manuscript included. 183pp. 6⅝ × 9⅝. 22384-1 Pa. $5.95

AUTOBIOGRAPHY: The Story of My Experiments with Truth, Mohandas K. Gandhi. Not hagiography, but Gandhi in his own words. Boyhood, legal studies, purification, the growth of the Satyagraha (nonviolent protest) movement. Critical, inspiring work of the man who freed India. 480pp. 5⅜ × 8½. (Available in U.S. only) 24593-4 Pa. $6.95

ILLUSTRATED DICTIONARY OF HISTORIC ARCHITECTURE, edited by Cyril M. Harris. Extraordinary compendium of clear, concise definitions for over 5,000 important architectural terms complemented by over 2,000 line drawings. Covers full spectrum of architecture from ancient ruins to 20th-century Modernism. Preface. 592pp. 7½ × 9⅜. 24444-X Pa. $15.95

THE NIGHT BEFORE CHRISTMAS, Clement C. Moore. Full text, and woodcuts from original 1848 book. Also critical, historical material. 19 illustrations. 40pp. 4⅝ × 6. 22797-9 Pa. $2.50

THE LESSON OF JAPANESE ARCHITECTURE: 165 Photographs, Jiro Harada. Memorable gallery of 165 photographs taken in the 1930s of exquisite Japanese homes of the well-to-do and historic buildings. 13 line diagrams. 192pp. 8⅜ × 11¼. 24778-3 Pa. $10.95

THE AUTOBIOGRAPHY OF CHARLES DARWIN AND SELECTED LETTERS, edited by Francis Darwin. The fascinating life of eccentric genius composed of an intimate memoir by Darwin (intended for his children); commentary by his son, Francis; hundreds of fragments from notebooks, journals, papers; and letters to and from Lyell, Hooker, Huxley, Wallace and Henslow. xi + 365pp. 5⅜ × 8. 20479-0 Pa. $6.95

WONDERS OF THE SKY: Observing Rainbows, Comets, Eclipses, the Stars and Other Phenomena, Fred Schaaf. Charming, easy-to-read poetic guide to all manner of celestial events visible to the naked eye. Mock suns, glories, Belt of Venus, more. Illustrated. 299pp. 5¼ × 8¼. 24402-4 Pa. $8.95

BURNHAM'S CELESTIAL HANDBOOK, Robert Burnham, Jr. Thorough guide to the stars beyond our solar system. Exhaustive treatment. Alphabetical by constellation: Andromeda to Cetus in Vol. 1; Chamaeleon to Orion in Vol. 2; and Pavo to Vulpecula in Vol. 3. Hundreds of illustrations. Index in Vol. 3. 2,000pp. 6⅛ × 9¼. 23567-X, 23568-8, 23673-0 Pa., Three-vol. set $41.85

STAR NAMES: Their Lore and Meaning, Richard Hinckley Allen. Fascinating history of names various cultures have given to constellations and literary and folkloristic uses that have been made of stars. Indexes to subjects. Arabic and Greek names. Biblical references. Bibliography. 563pp. 5⅜ × 8½. 21079-0 Pa. $8.95

THIRTY YEARS THAT SHOOK PHYSICS: The Story of Quantum Theory, George Gamow. Lucid, accessible introduction to influential theory of energy and matter. Careful explanations of Dirac's anti-particles, Bohr's model of the atom, much more. 12 plates. Numerous drawings. 240pp. 5⅜ × 8½. 24895-X Pa. $6.95

CHINESE DOMESTIC FURNITURE IN PHOTOGRAPHS AND MEASURED DRAWINGS, Gustav Ecke. A rare volume, now affordably priced for antique collectors, furniture buffs and art historians. Detailed review of styles ranging from early Shang to late Ming. Unabridged republication. 161 black-and-white drawings, photos. Total of 224pp. 8⅜ × 11¼. (Available in U.S. only) 25171-3 Pa. $14.95

VINCENT VAN GOGH: A Biography, Julius Meier-Graefe. Dynamic, penetrating study of artist's life, relationship with brother, Theo, painting techniques, travels, more. Readable, engrossing. 160pp. 5⅜ × 8½. (Available in U.S. only) 25253-1 Pa. $4.95

HOW TO WRITE, Gertrude Stein. Gertrude Stein claimed anyone could understand her unconventional writing—here are clues to help. Fascinating improvisations, language experiments, explanations illuminate Stein's craft and the art of writing. Total of 414pp. 4⅜ × 6⅜. 23144-5 Pa. $6.95

ADVENTURES AT SEA IN THE GREAT AGE OF SAIL: Five Firsthand Narratives, edited by Elliot Snow. Rare true accounts of exploration, whaling, shipwreck, fierce natives, trade, shipboard life, more. 33 illustrations. Introduction. 353pp. 5⅜ × 8½. 25177-2 Pa. $9.95

THE HERBAL OR GENERAL HISTORY OF PLANTS, John Gerard. Classic descriptions of about 2,850 plants—with over 2,700 illustrations—includes Latin and English names, physical descriptions, varieties, time and place of growth, more. 2,706 illustrations. xlv + 1,678pp. 8½ × 12¼. 23147-X Cloth. $75.00

DOROTHY AND THE WIZARD IN OZ, L. Frank Baum. Dorothy and the Wizard visit the center of the Earth, where people are vegetables, glass houses grow and Oz characters reappear. Classic sequel to *Wizard of Oz*. 256pp. 5⅜ × 8. 24714-7 Pa. $5.95

SONGS OF EXPERIENCE: Facsimile Reproduction with 26 Plates in Full Color, William Blake. This facsimile of Blake's original "Illuminated Book" reproduces 26 full-color plates from a rare 1826 edition. Includes "The Tyger," "London," "Holy Thursday," and other immortal poems. 26 color plates. Printed text of poems. 48pp. 5¼ × 7. 24636-1 Pa. $3.95

SONGS OF INNOCENCE, William Blake. The first and most popular of Blake's famous "Illuminated Books," in a facsimile edition reproducing all 31 brightly colored plates. Additional printed text of each poem. 64pp. 5¼ × 7. 22764-2 Pa. $3.95

PRECIOUS STONES, Max Bauer. Classic, thorough study of diamonds, rubies, emeralds, garnets, etc.: physical character, occurrence, properties, use, similar topics. 20 plates, 8 in color. 94 figures. 659pp. 6⅛ × 9¼. 21910-0, 21911-9 Pa., Two-vol. set $15.90

ENCYCLOPEDIA OF VICTORIAN NEEDLEWORK, S. F. A. Caulfeild and Blanche Saward. Full, precise descriptions of stitches, techniques for dozens of needlecrafts—most exhaustive reference of its kind. Over 800 figures. Total of 679pp. 8⅛ × 11. 22800-2, 22801-0 Pa., Two-vol. set $23.90

THE MARVELOUS LAND OF OZ, L. Frank Baum. Second Oz book, the Scarecrow and Tin Woodman are back with hero named Tip, Oz magic. 136 illustrations. 287pp. 5⅜ × 8½. 20692-0 Pa. $5.95

WILD FOWL DECOYS, Joel Barber. Basic book on the subject, by foremost authority and collector. Reveals history of decoy making and rigging, place in American culture, different kinds of decoys, how to make them, and how to use them. 140 plates. 156pp. 7⅞ × 10¾. 20011-6 Pa. $8.95

HISTORY OF LACE, Mrs. Bury Palliser. Definitive, profusely illustrated chronicle of lace from earliest times to late 19th century. Laces of Italy, Greece, England, France, Belgium, etc. Landmark of needlework scholarship. 266 illustrations. 672pp. 6⅛ × 9¼. 24742-2 Pa. $16.95

ILLUSTRATED GUIDE TO SHAKER FURNITURE, Robert Meader. All furniture and appurtenances, with much on unknown local styles. 235 photos. 146pp. 9 × 12. 22819-3 Pa. $8.95

WHALE SHIPS AND WHALING: A Pictorial Survey, George Francis Dow. Over 200 vintage engravings, drawings, photographs of barks, brigs, cutters, other vessels. Also harpoons, lances, whaling guns, many other artifacts. Comprehensive text by foremost authority. 207 black-and-white illustrations. 288pp. 6 × 9.
24808-9 Pa. $9.95

THE BERTRAMS, Anthony Trollope. Powerful portrayal of blind self-will and thwarted ambition includes one of Trollope's most heartrending love stories. 497pp. 5⅜ × 8½. 25119-5 Pa. $9.95

ADVENTURES WITH A HAND LENS, Richard Headstrom. Clearly written guide to observing and studying flowers and grasses, fish scales, moth and insect wings, egg cases, buds, feathers, seeds, leaf scars, moss, molds, ferns, common crystals, etc.—all with an ordinary, inexpensive magnifying glass. 209 exact line drawings aid in your discoveries. 220pp. 5⅜ × 8½. 23330-8 Pa. $5.95

RODIN ON ART AND ARTISTS, Auguste Rodin. Great sculptor's candid, wide-ranging comments on meaning of art; great artists; relation of sculpture to poetry, painting, music; philosophy of life, more. 76 superb black-and-white illustrations of Rodin's sculpture, drawings and prints. 119pp. 8⅜ × 11¼. 24487-3 Pa. $7.95

FIFTY CLASSIC FRENCH FILMS, 1912–1982: A Pictorial Record, Anthony Slide. Memorable stills from Grand Illusion, Beauty and the Beast, Hiroshima, Mon Amour, many more. Credits, plot synopses, reviews, etc. 160pp. 8¼ × 11.
25256-6 Pa. $11.95

THE PRINCIPLES OF PSYCHOLOGY, William James. Famous long course complete, unabridged. Stream of thought, time perception, memory, experimental methods; great work decades ahead of its time. 94 figures. 1,391pp. 5⅜ × 8½.
20381-6, 20382-4 Pa., Two-vol. set $25.90

BODIES IN A BOOKSHOP, R. T. Campbell. Challenging mystery of blackmail and murder with ingenious plot and superbly drawn characters. In the best tradition of British suspense fiction. 192pp. 5⅜ × 8½. 24720-1 Pa. $4.95

CALLAS: Portrait of a Prima Donna, George Jellinek. Renowned commentator on the musical scene chronicles incredible career and life of the most controversial, fascinating, influential operatic personality of our time. 64 black-and-white photographs. 416pp. 5⅜ × 8¼. 25047-4 Pa. $8.95

GEOMETRY, RELATIVITY AND THE FOURTH DIMENSION, Rudolph Rucker. Exposition of fourth dimension, concepts of relativity as Flatland characters continue adventures. Popular, easily followed yet accurate, profound. 141 illustrations. 133pp. 5⅜ × 8½. 23400-2 Pa. $4.95

HOUSEHOLD STORIES BY THE BROTHERS GRIMM, with pictures by Walter Crane. 53 classic stories—Rumpelstiltskin, Rapunzel, Hansel and Gretel, the Fisherman and his Wife, Snow White, Tom Thumb, Sleeping Beauty, Cinderella, and so much more—lavishly illustrated with original 19th-century drawings. 114 illustrations. x + 269pp. 5⅜ × 8½. 21080-4 Pa. $4.95

SUNDIALS, Albert Waugh. Far and away the best, most thorough coverage of ideas, mathematics concerned, types, construction, adjusting anywhere. Over 100 illustrations. 230pp. 5⅜ × 8½. 22947-5 Pa. $5.95

PICTURE HISTORY OF THE NORMANDIE: With 190 Illustrations, Frank O. Braynard. Full story of legendary French ocean liner: Art Deco interiors, design innovations, furnishings, celebrities, maiden voyage, tragic fire, much more. Extensive text. 144pp. 8⅞ × 11¾. 25257-4 Pa. $10.95

THE FIRST AMERICAN COOKBOOK: A Facsimile of "American Cookery," 1796, Amelia Simmons. Facsimile of the first American-written cookbook published in the United States contains authentic recipes for colonial favorites—pumpkin pudding, winter squash pudding, spruce beer, Indian slapjacks, and more. Introductory Essay and Glossary of colonial cooking terms. 80pp. 5⅜ × 8½. 24710-4 Pa. $3.50

101 PUZZLES IN THOUGHT AND LOGIC, C. R. Wylie, Jr. Solve murders and robberies, find out which fishermen are liars, how a blind man could possibly identify a color—purely by your own reasoning! 107pp. 5⅜ × 8½. 20367-0 Pa. $2.95

ANCIENT EGYPTIAN MYTHS AND LEGENDS, Lewis Spence. Examines animism, totemism, fetishism, creation myths, deities, alchemy, art and magic, other topics. Over 50 illustrations. 432pp. 5⅜ × 8½. 26525-0 Pa. $8.95

ANTHROPOLOGY AND MODERN LIFE, Franz Boas. Great anthropologist's classic treatise on race and culture. Introduction by Ruth Bunzel. Only inexpensive paperback edition. 255pp. 5⅜ × 8½. 25245-0 Pa. $6.95

THE TALE OF PETER RABBIT, Beatrix Potter. The inimitable Peter's terrifying adventure in Mr. McGregor's garden, with all 27 wonderful, full-color Potter illustrations. 55pp. 4¼ × 5½. (Available in U.S. only) 22827-4 Pa. $1.75

THREE PROPHETIC SCIENCE FICTION NOVELS, H. G. Wells. *When the Sleeper Wakes, A Story of the Days to Come* and *The Time Machine* (full version). 335pp. 5⅜ × 8½. (Available in U.S. only) 20605-X Pa. $8.95

APICIUS COOKERY AND DINING IN IMPERIAL ROME, edited and translated by Joseph Dommers Vehling. Oldest known cookbook in existence offers readers a clear picture of what foods Romans ate, how they prepared them, etc. 49 illustrations. 301pp. 6⅛ × 9¼. 23563-7 Pa. $7.95

SHAKESPEARE LEXICON AND QUOTATION DICTIONARY, Alexander Schmidt. Full definitions, locations, shades of meaning of every word in plays and poems. More than 50,000 exact quotations. 1,485pp. 6½ × 9¼. 22726-X, 22727-8 Pa., Two-vol. set $31.90

THE WORLD'S GREAT SPEECHES, edited by Lewis Copeland and Lawrence W. Lamm. Vast collection of 278 speeches from Greeks to 1970. Powerful and effective models; unique look at history. 842pp. 5⅜ × 8½. 20468-5 Pa. $12.95

THE BLUE FAIRY BOOK, Andrew Lang. The first, most famous collection, with many familiar tales: Little Red Riding Hood, Aladdin and the Wonderful Lamp, Puss in Boots, Sleeping Beauty, Hansel and Gretel, Rumpelstiltskin; 37 in all. 138 illustrations. 390pp. 5⅜ × 8½.   21437-0 Pa. $6.95

THE STORY OF THE CHAMPIONS OF THE ROUND TABLE, Howard Pyle. Sir Launcelot, Sir Tristram and Sir Percival in spirited adventures of love and triumph retold in Pyle's inimitable style. 50 drawings, 31 full-page. xviii + 329pp. 6½ × 9¼.   21883-X Pa. $7.95

THE MYTHS OF THE NORTH AMERICAN INDIANS, Lewis Spence. Myths and legends of the Algonquins, Iroquois, Pawnees and Sioux with comprehensive historical and ethnological commentary. 36 illustrations. 5⅜ × 8½.
25967-6 Pa. $8.95

GREAT DINOSAUR HUNTERS AND THEIR DISCOVERIES, Edwin H. Colbert. Fascinating, lavishly illustrated chronicle of dinosaur research, 1820s to 1960. Achievements of Cope, Marsh, Brown, Buckland, Mantell, Huxley, many others. 384pp. 5¼ × 8¼.   24701-5 Pa. $7.95

THE TASTEMAKERS, Russell Lynes. Informal, illustrated social history of American taste 1850s–1950s. First popularized categories Highbrow, Lowbrow, Middlebrow. 129 illustrations. New (1979) afterword. 384pp. 6 × 9.
23993-4 Pa. $8.95

DOUBLE CROSS PURPOSES, Ronald A. Knox. A treasure hunt in the Scottish Highlands, an old map, unidentified corpse, surprise discoveries keep reader guessing in this cleverly intricate tale of financial skullduggery. 2 black-and-white maps. 320pp. 5⅜ × 8½. (Available in U.S. only)   25032-6 Pa. $6.95

AUTHENTIC VICTORIAN DECORATION AND ORNAMENTATION IN FULL COLOR: 46 Plates from "Studies in Design," Christopher Dresser. Superb full-color lithographs reproduced from rare original portfolio of a major Victorian designer. 48pp. 9¼ × 12¼.   25083-0 Pa. $7.95

PRIMITIVE ART, Franz Boas. Remains the best text ever prepared on subject, thoroughly discussing Indian, African, Asian, Australian, and, especially, Northern American primitive art. Over 950 illustrations show ceramics, masks, totem poles, weapons, textiles, paintings, much more. 376pp. 5⅜ × 8.   20025-6 Pa. $7.95

SIDELIGHTS ON RELATIVITY, Albert Einstein. Unabridged republication of two lectures delivered by the great physicist in 1920–21. *Ether and Relativity* and *Geometry and Experience*. Elegant ideas in nonmathematical form, accessible to intelligent layman. vi + 56pp. 5⅜ × 8½.   24511-X Pa. $3.95

THE WIT AND HUMOR OF OSCAR WILDE, edited by Alvin Redman. More than 1,000 ripostes, paradoxes, wisecracks: Work is the curse of the drinking classes, I can resist everything except temptation, etc. 258pp. 5⅜ × 8½.   20602-5 Pa. $4.95

ADVENTURES WITH A MICROSCOPE, Richard Headstrom. 59 adventures with clothing fibers, protozoa, ferns and lichens, roots and leaves, much more. 142 illustrations. 232pp. 5⅜ × 8½.   23471-1 Pa. $3.95

PLANTS OF THE BIBLE, Harold N. Moldenke and Alma L. Moldenke. Standard reference to all 230 plants mentioned in Scriptures. Latin name, biblical reference, uses, modern identity, much more. Unsurpassed encyclopedic resource for scholars, botanists, nature lovers, students of Bible. Bibliography. Indexes. 123 black-and-white illustrations. 384pp. 6 × 9. 25069-5 Pa. $8.95

FAMOUS AMERICAN WOMEN: A Biographical Dictionary from Colonial Times to the Present, Robert McHenry, ed. From Pocahontas to Rosa Parks, 1,035 distinguished American women documented in separate biographical entries. Accurate, up-to-date data, numerous categories, spans 400 years. Indices. 493pp. 6½ × 9¼. 24523-3 Pa. $10.95

THE FABULOUS INTERIORS OF THE GREAT OCEAN LINERS IN HISTORIC PHOTOGRAPHS, William H. Miller, Jr. Some 200 superb photographs capture exquisite interiors of world's great "floating palaces"—1890s to 1980s: *Titanic, Ile de France, Queen Elizabeth, United States, Europa,* more. Approx. 200 black-and-white photographs. Captions. Text. Introduction. 160pp. 8⅞ × 11¾. 24756-2 Pa. $9.95

THE GREAT LUXURY LINERS, 1927–1954: A Photographic Record, William H. Miller, Jr. Nostalgic tribute to heyday of ocean liners. 186 photos of *Ile de France, Normandie, Leviathan, Queen Elizabeth, United States,* many others. Interior and exterior views. Introduction. Captions. 160pp. 9 × 12. 24056-8 Pa. $10.95

A NATURAL HISTORY OF THE DUCKS, John Charles Phillips. Great landmark of ornithology offers complete detailed coverage of nearly 200 species and subspecies of ducks: gadwall, sheldrake, merganser, pintail, many more. 74 full-color plates, 102 black-and-white. Bibliography. Total of 1,920pp. 8⅜ × 11¼. 25141-1, 25142-X Cloth., Two-vol. set $100.00

THE SEAWEED HANDBOOK: An Illustrated Guide to Seaweeds from North Carolina to Canada, Thomas F. Lee. Concise reference covers 78 species. Scientific and common names, habitat, distribution, more. Finding keys for easy identification. 224pp. 5⅜ × 8½. 25215-9 Pa. $6.95

THE TEN BOOKS OF ARCHITECTURE: The 1755 Leoni Edition, Leon Battista Alberti. Rare classic helped introduce the glories of ancient architecture to the Renaissance. 68 black-and-white plates. 336pp. 8⅜ × 11¼. 25239-6 Pa. $14.95

MISS MACKENZIE, Anthony Trollope. Minor masterpieces by Victorian master unmasks many truths about life in 19th-century England. First inexpensive edition in years. 392pp. 5⅜ × 8½. 25201-9 Pa. $8.95

THE RIME OF THE ANCIENT MARINER, Gustave Doré, Samuel Taylor Coleridge. Dramatic engravings considered by many to be his greatest work. The terrifying space of the open sea, the storms and whirlpools of an unknown ocean, the ice of Antarctica, more—all rendered in a powerful, chilling manner. Full text. 38 plates. 77pp. 9¼ × 12. 22305-1 Pa. $4.95

THE EXPEDITIONS OF ZEBULON MONTGOMERY PIKE, Zebulon Montgomery Pike. Fascinating firsthand accounts (1805–6) of exploration of Mississippi River, Indian wars, capture by Spanish dragoons, much more. 1,088pp. 5⅜ × 8½. 25254-X, 25255-8 Pa., Two-vol. set $25.90

CATALOG OF DOVER BOOKS

A CONCISE HISTORY OF PHOTOGRAPHY: Third Revised Edition, Helmut Gernsheim. Best one-volume history—camera obscura, photochemistry, daguerreotypes, evolution of cameras, film, more. Also artistic aspects—landscape, portraits, fine art, etc. 281 black-and-white photographs. 26 in color. 176pp. 8⅜ × 11¼. 25128-4 Pa. $14.95

THE DORÉ BIBLE ILLUSTRATIONS, Gustave Doré. 241 detailed plates from the Bible: the Creation scenes, Adam and Eve, Flood, Babylon, battle sequences, life of Jesus, etc. Each plate is accompanied by the verses from the King James version of the Bible. 241pp. 9 × 12. 23004-X Pa. $9.95

WANDERINGS IN WEST AFRICA, Richard F. Burton. Great Victorian scholar/adventurer's invaluable descriptions of African tribal rituals, fetishism, culture, art, much more. Fascinating 19th-century account. 624pp. 5⅜ × 8½. 26890-X Pa. $12.95

FLATLAND, E. A. Abbott. Intriguing and enormously popular science-fiction classic explores the complexities of trying to survive as a two-dimensional being in a three-dimensional world. Amusingly illustrated by the author. 16 illustrations. 103pp. 5⅜ × 8½. 20001-9 Pa. $2.50

THE HISTORY OF THE LEWIS AND CLARK EXPEDITION, Meriwether Lewis and William Clark, edited by Elliott Coues. Classic edition of Lewis and Clark's day-by-day journals that later became the basis for U.S. claims to Oregon and the West. Accurate and invaluable geographical, botanical, biological, meteorological and anthropological material. Total of 1,508pp. 5⅜ × 8½. 21268-8, 21269-6, 21270-X Pa., Three-vol. set $29.85

LANGUAGE, TRUTH AND LOGIC, Alfred J. Ayer. Famous, clear introduction to Vienna, Cambridge schools of Logical Positivism. Role of philosophy, elimination of metaphysics, nature of analysis, etc. 160pp. 5⅜ × 8½. (Available in U.S. and Canada only) 20010-8 Pa. $3.95

MATHEMATICS FOR THE NONMATHEMATICIAN, Morris Kline. Detailed, college-level treatment of mathematics in cultural and historical context, with numerous exercises. For liberal arts students. Preface. Recommended Reading Lists. Tables. Index. Numerous black-and-white figures. xvi + 641pp. 5⅜ × 8½. 24823-2 Pa. $11.95

HANDBOOK OF PICTORIAL SYMBOLS, Rudolph Modley. 3,250 signs and symbols, many systems in full; official or heavy commercial use. Arranged by subject. Most in Pictorial Archive series. 143pp. 8⅛ × 11. 23357-X Pa. $7.95

INCIDENTS OF TRAVEL IN YUCATAN, John L. Stephens. Classic (1843) exploration of jungles of Yucatan, looking for evidences of Maya civilization. Travel adventures, Mexican and Indian culture, etc. Total of 669pp. 5⅜ × 8½. 20926-1, 20927-X Pa., Two-vol. set $11.90

DEGAS: An Intimate Portrait, Ambroise Vollard. Charming, anecdotal memoir by famous art dealer of one of the greatest 19th-century French painters. 14 black-and-white illustrations. Introduction by Harold L. Van Doren. 96pp. 5⅜ × 8½.
25131-4 Pa. $4.95

PERSONAL NARRATIVE OF A PILGRIMAGE TO AL-MADINAH AND MECCAH, Richard F. Burton. Great travel classic by remarkably colorful personality. Burton, disguised as a Moroccan, visited sacred shrines of Islam, narrowly escaping death. 47 illustrations. 959pp. 5⅜ × 8½.
21217-3, 21218-1 Pa., Two-vol. set $19.90

PHRASE AND WORD ORIGINS, A. H. Holt. Entertaining, reliable, modern study of more than 1,200 colorful words, phrases, origins and histories. Much unexpected information. 254pp. 5⅜ × 8½.
20758-7 Pa. $5.95

THE RED THUMB MARK, R. Austin Freeman. In this first Dr. Thorndyke case, the great scientific detective draws fascinating conclusions from the nature of a single fingerprint. Exciting story, authentic science. 320pp. 5⅜ × 8½. (Available in U.S. only)
25210-8 Pa. $6.95

AN EGYPTIAN HIEROGLYPHIC DICTIONARY, E. A. Wallis Budge. Monumental work containing about 25,000 words or terms that occur in texts ranging from 3000 B.C. to 600 A.D. Each entry consists of a transliteration of the word, the word in hieroglyphs, and the meaning in English. 1,314pp. 6⅜ × 10.
23615-3, 23616-1 Pa., Two-vol. set $35.90

THE COMPLEAT STRATEGYST: Being a Primer on the Theory of Games of Strategy, J. D. Williams. Highly entertaining classic describes, with many illustrated examples, how to select best strategies in conflict situations. Prefaces. Appendices. xvi + 268pp. 5⅜ × 8½.
25101-2 Pa. $6.95

THE ROAD TO OZ, L. Frank Baum. Dorothy meets the Shaggy Man, little Button-Bright and the Rainbow's beautiful daughter in this delightful trip to the magical Land of Oz. 272pp. 5⅜ × 8.
25208-6 Pa. $5.95

POINT AND LINE TO PLANE, Wassily Kandinsky. Seminal exposition of role of point, line, other elements in nonobjective painting. Essential to understanding 20th-century art. 127 illustrations. 192pp. 6½ × 9¼.
23808-3 Pa. $5.95

LADY ANNA, Anthony Trollope. Moving chronicle of Countess Lovel's bitter struggle to win for herself and daughter Anna their rightful rank and fortune—perhaps at cost of sanity itself. 384pp. 5⅜ × 8½.
24669-8 Pa. $8.95

EGYPTIAN MAGIC, E. A. Wallis Budge. Sums up all that is known about magic in Ancient Egypt: the role of magic in controlling the gods, powerful amulets that warded off evil spirits, scarabs of immortality, use of wax images, formulas and spells, the secret name, much more. 253pp. 5⅜ × 8½.
22681-6 Pa. $4.50

THE DANCE OF SIVA, Ananda Coomaraswamy. Preeminent authority unfolds the vast metaphysic of India: the revelation of her art, conception of the universe, social organization, etc. 27 reproductions of art masterpieces. 192pp. 5⅜ × 8½.
24817-8 Pa. $6.95

CHRISTMAS CUSTOMS AND TRADITIONS, Clement A. Miles. Origin, evolution, significance of religious, secular practices. Caroling, gifts, yule logs, much more. Full, scholarly yet fascinating; non-sectarian. 400pp. 5⅜ × 8½.
23354-5 Pa. $6.95

THE HUMAN FIGURE IN MOTION, Eadweard Muybridge. More than 4,500 stopped-action photos, in action series, showing undraped men, women, children jumping, lying down, throwing, sitting, wrestling, carrying, etc. 390pp. 7⅞ × 10⅝.
20204-6 Cloth. $24.95

THE MAN WHO WAS THURSDAY, Gilbert Keith Chesterton. Witty, fast-paced novel about a club of anarchists in turn-of-the-century London. Brilliant social, religious, philosophical speculations. 128pp. 5⅜ × 8½.
25121-7 Pa. $3.95

A CÉZANNE SKETCHBOOK: Figures, Portraits, Landscapes and Still Lifes, Paul Cézanne. Great artist experiments with tonal effects, light, mass, other qualities in over 100 drawings. A revealing view of developing master painter, precursor of Cubism. 102 black-and-white illustrations. 144pp. 8¾ × 6⅝.
24790-2 Pa. $6.95

AN ENCYCLOPEDIA OF BATTLES: Accounts of Over 1,560 Battles from 1479 B.C. to the Present, David Eggenberger. Presents essential details of every major battle in recorded history, from the first battle of Megiddo in 1479 B.C. to Grenada in 1984. List of Battle Maps. New Appendix covering the years 1967–1984. Index. 99 illustrations. 544pp. 6½ × 9¼.
24913-1 Pa. $14.95

AN ETYMOLOGICAL DICTIONARY OF MODERN ENGLISH, Ernest Weekley. Richest, fullest work, by foremost British lexicographer. Detailed word histories. Inexhaustible. Total of 856pp. 6½ × 9¼.
21873-2, 21874-0 Pa., Two-vol. set $19.90

WEBSTER'S AMERICAN MILITARY BIOGRAPHIES, edited by Robert McHenry. Over 1,000 figures who shaped 3 centuries of American military history. Detailed biographies of Nathan Hale, Douglas MacArthur, Mary Hallaren, others. Chronologies of engagements, more. Introduction. Addenda. 1,033 entries in alphabetical order. xi + 548pp. 6½ × 9¼. (Available in U.S. only)
24758-9 Pa. $13.95

LIFE IN ANCIENT EGYPT, Adolf Erman. Detailed older account, with much not in more recent books: domestic life, religion, magic, medicine, commerce, and whatever else needed for complete picture. Many illustrations. 597pp. 5⅜ × 8½.
22632-8 Pa. $8.95

HISTORIC COSTUME IN PICTURES, Braun & Schneider. Over 1,450 costumed figures shown, covering a wide variety of peoples: kings, emperors, nobles, priests, servants, soldiers, scholars, townsfolk, peasants, merchants, courtiers, cavaliers, and more. 256pp. 8⅜ × 11¼.
23150-X Pa. $9.95

THE NOTEBOOKS OF LEONARDO DA VINCI, edited by J. P. Richter. Extracts from manuscripts reveal great genius; on painting, sculpture, anatomy, sciences, geography, etc. Both Italian and English. 186 ms. pages reproduced, plus 500 additional drawings, including studies for *Last Supper*, *Sforza* monument, etc. 860pp. 7⅞ × 10¾. (Available in U.S. only) 22572-0, 22573-9 Pa., Two-vol. set $31.90

CATALOG OF DOVER BOOKS

THE ART NOUVEAU STYLE BOOK OF ALPHONSE MUCHA: All 72 Plates from "Documents Decoratifs" in Original Color, Alphonse Mucha. Rare copyright-free design portfolio by high priest of Art Nouveau. Jewelry, wallpaper, stained glass, furniture, figure studies, plant and animal motifs, etc. Only complete one-volume edition. 80pp. 9⅜ × 12¼. 24044-4 Pa. $10.95

ANIMALS: 1,419 Copyright-Free Illustrations of Mammals, Birds, Fish, Insects, Etc., edited by Jim Harter. Clear wood engravings present, in extremely lifelike poses, over 1,000 species of animals. One of the most extensive pictorial sourcebooks of its kind. Captions. Index. 284pp. 9 × 12. 23766-4 Pa. $10.95

OBELISTS FLY HIGH, C. Daly King. Masterpiece of American detective fiction, long out of print, involves murder on a 1935 transcontinental flight—"a very thrilling story"—NY Times. Unabridged and unaltered republication of the edition published by William Collins Sons & Co. Ltd., London, 1935. 288pp. 5⅜ × 8½. (Available in U.S. only) 25036-9 Pa. $5.95

VICTORIAN AND EDWARDIAN FASHION: A Photographic Survey, Alison Gernsheim. First fashion history completely illustrated by contemporary photographs. Full text plus 235 photos, 1840–1914, in which many celebrities appear. 240pp. 6½ × 9¼. 24205-6 Pa. $8.95

THE ART OF THE FRENCH ILLUSTRATED BOOK, 1700–1914, Gordon N. Ray. Over 630 superb book illustrations by Fragonard, Delacroix, Daumier, Doré, Grandville, Manet, Mucha, Steinlen, Toulouse-Lautrec and many others. Preface. Introduction. 633 halftones. Indices of artists, authors & titles, binders and provenances. Appendices. Bibliography. 608pp. 8⅜ × 11¼. 25086-5 Pa. $24.95

THE WONDERFUL WIZARD OF OZ, L. Frank Baum. Facsimile in full color of America's finest children's classic. 143 illustrations by W. W. Denslow. 267pp. 5⅜ × 8½. 20691-2 Pa. $7.95

FOLLOWING THE EQUATOR: A Journey Around the World, Mark Twain. Great writer's 1897 account of circumnavigating the globe by steamship. Ironic humor, keen observations, vivid and fascinating descriptions of exotic places. 197 illustrations. 720pp. 5⅜ × 8½. 26113-1 Pa. $15.95

THE FRIENDLY STARS, Martha Evans Martin & Donald Howard Menzel. Classic text marshalls the stars together in an engaging, nontechnical survey, presenting them as sources of beauty in night sky. 23 illustrations. Foreword. 2 star charts. Index. 147pp. 5⅜ × 8½. 21099-5 Pa. $3.95

FADS AND FALLACIES IN THE NAME OF SCIENCE, Martin Gardner. Fair, witty appraisal of cranks, quacks, and quackeries of science and pseudoscience: hollow earth, Velikovsky, orgone energy, Dianetics, flying saucers, Bridey Murphy, food and medical fads, etc. Revised, expanded In the Name of Science. "A very able and even-tempered presentation."—The New Yorker. 363pp. 5⅜ × 8. 20394-8 Pa. $6.95

ANCIENT EGYPT: Its Culture and History, J. E. Manchip White. From predynastics through Ptolemies: society, history, political structure, religion, daily life, literature, cultural heritage. 48 plates. 217pp. 5⅜ × 8½. 22548-8 Pa. $5.95

CATALOG OF DOVER BOOKS

SIR HARRY HOTSPUR OF HUMBLETHWAITE, Anthony Trollope. Incisive, unconventional psychological study of a conflict between a wealthy baronet, his idealistic daughter, and their scapegrace cousin. The 1870 novel in its first inexpensive edition in years. 250pp. 5⅜ × 8½.   24953-0 Pa. $6.95

LASERS AND HOLOGRAPHY, Winston E. Kock. Sound introduction to burgeoning field, expanded (1981) for second edition. Wave patterns, coherence, lasers, diffraction, zone plates, properties of holograms, recent advances. 84 illustrations. 160pp. 5⅜ × 8¼. (Except in United Kingdom)   24041-X Pa. $3.95

INTRODUCTION TO ARTIFICIAL INTELLIGENCE: Second, Enlarged Edition, Philip C. Jackson, Jr. Comprehensive survey of artificial intelligence—the study of how machines (computers) can be made to act intelligently. Includes introductory and advanced material. Extensive notes updating the main text. 132 black-and-white illustrations. 512pp. 5⅜ × 8½.   24864-X Pa. $10.95

HISTORY OF INDIAN AND INDONESIAN ART, Ananda K. Coomaraswamy. Over 400 illustrations illuminate classic study of Indian art from earliest Harappa finds to early 20th century. Provides philosophical, religious and social insights. 304pp. 6⅜ × 9⅜.   25005-9 Pa. $11.95

THE GOLEM, Gustav Meyrink. Most famous supernatural novel in modern European literature, set in Ghetto of Old Prague around 1890. Compelling story of mystical experiences, strange transformations, profound terror. 13 black-and-white illustrations. 224pp. 5⅜ × 8½. (Available in U.S. only)   25025-3 Pa. $6.95

PICTORIAL ENCYCLOPEDIA OF HISTORIC ARCHITECTURAL PLANS, DETAILS AND ELEMENTS: With 1,880 Line Drawings of Arches, Domes, Doorways, Facades, Gables, Windows, etc., John Theodore Haneman. Sourcebook of inspiration for architects, designers, others. Bibliography. Captions. 141pp. 9 × 12.   24605-1 Pa. $7.95

BENCHLEY LOST AND FOUND, Robert Benchley. Finest humor from early 30s, about pet peeves, child psychologists, post office and others. Mostly unavailable elsewhere. 73 illustrations by Peter Arno and others. 183pp. 5⅜ × 8½.   22410-4 Pa. $4.95

ERTÉ GRAPHICS, Erté. Collection of striking color graphics: *Seasons, Alphabet, Numerals, Aces* and *Precious Stones*. 50 plates, including 4 on covers. 48pp. 9⅜ × 12¼.   23580-7 Pa. $7.95

THE JOURNAL OF HENRY D. THOREAU, edited by Bradford Torrey, F. H. Allen. Complete reprinting of 14 volumes, 1837–61, over two million words; the sourcebooks for *Walden*, etc. Definitive. All original sketches, plus 75 photographs. 1,804pp. 8½ × 12¼.   20312-3, 20313-1 Cloth., Two-vol. set $130.00

CASTLES: Their Construction and History, Sidney Toy. Traces castle development from ancient roots. Nearly 200 photographs and drawings illustrate moats, keeps, baileys, many other features. Caernarvon, Dover Castles, Hadrian's Wall, Tower of London, dozens more. 256pp. 5⅜ × 8¼.   24898-4 Pa. $6.95

AMERICAN CLIPPER SHIPS: 1833–1858, Octavius T. Howe & Frederick C. Matthews. Fully-illustrated, encyclopedic review of 352 clipper ships from the period of America's greatest maritime supremacy. Introduction. 109 halftones. 5 black-and-white line illustrations. Index. Total of 928pp. 5⅜ × 8½.
25115-2, 25116-0 Pa., Two-vol. set $17.90

TOWARDS A NEW ARCHITECTURE, Le Corbusier. Pioneering manifesto by great architect, near legendary founder of "International School." Technical and aesthetic theories, views on industry, economics, relation of form to function, "mass-production spirit," much more. Profusely illustrated. Unabridged translation of 13th French edition. Introduction by Frederick Etchells. 320pp. 6⅛ × 9¼. (Available in U.S. only)
25023-7 Pa. $8.95

THE BOOK OF KELLS, edited by Blanche Cirker. Inexpensive collection of 32 full-color, full-page plates from the greatest illuminated manuscript of the Middle Ages, painstakingly reproduced from rare facsimile edition. Publisher's Note. Captions. 32pp. 9⅜ × 12¼.
24345-1 Pa. $5.95

BEST SCIENCE FICTION STORIES OF H. G. WELLS, H. G. Wells. Full novel *The Invisible Man*, plus 17 short stories: "The Crystal Egg," "Aepyornis Island," "The Strange Orchid," etc. 303pp. 5⅜ × 8½. (Available in U.S. only)
21531-8 Pa. $6.95

AMERICAN SAILING SHIPS: Their Plans and History, Charles G. Davis. Photos, construction details of schooners, frigates, clippers, other sailcraft of 18th to early 20th centuries—plus entertaining discourse on design, rigging, nautical lore, much more. 137 black-and-white illustrations. 240pp. 6⅛ × 9¼.
24658-2 Pa. $6.95

ENTERTAINING MATHEMATICAL PUZZLES, Martin Gardner. Selection of author's favorite conundrums involving arithmetic, money, speed, etc., with lively commentary. Complete solutions. 112pp. 5⅜ × 8½.
25211-6 Pa. $3.50

THE WILL TO BELIEVE, HUMAN IMMORTALITY, William James. Two books bound together. Effect of irrational on logical, and arguments for human immortality. 402pp. 5⅜ × 8½.
20291-7 Pa. $8.95

THE HAUNTED MONASTERY and THE CHINESE MAZE MURDERS, Robert Van Gulik. 2 full novels by Van Gulik continue adventures of Judge Dee and his companions. An evil Taoist monastery, seemingly supernatural events; overgrown topiary maze that hides strange crimes. Set in 7th-century China. 27 illustrations. 328pp. 5⅜ × 8½.
23502-5 Pa. $6.95

CELEBRATED CASES OF JUDGE DEE (DEE GOONG AN), translated by Robert Van Gulik. Authentic 18th-century Chinese detective novel; Dee and associates solve three interlocked cases. Led to Van Gulik's own stories with same characters. Extensive introduction. 9 illustrations. 237pp. 5⅜ × 8½.
23337-5 Pa. $5.95

Prices subject to change without notice.

Available at your book dealer or write for free catalog to Dept. GI, Dover Publications, Inc., 31 East 2nd St., Mineola, N.Y. 11501. Dover publishes more than 175 books each year on science, elementary and advanced mathematics, biology, music, art, literary history, social sciences and other areas.